THE SUNDAY SERIES
WITH MARK BRODINSKY

Real Stories of Courage, Hope & Inspiration

Volume 1

Mark Brodinsky

THE SUNDAY SERIES WITH MARK BRODINSKY:

Dedication

The Sunday Series is truly a labor of love in my life.

This Volume I, the beginning of it all, is dedicated to the young man whose life ended much too soon. Ian's Story - the first of this series – is why and how this all began. But this is just one tiny piece of the huge impact Ian Scher had on all he touched.

April 2017, the month this book is published, would have been the month Ian turned 14.

His family always knew there would be a premature end to Ian's physical journey here on this earth – but his heart, his spirit and his superhero powers live on forever.

Rest in Peace Spiderman.

Love,

Mark Brodinsky

TABLE OF CONTENTS

Acknowledgements

Where do you begin?

That's easy – start by thanking all who had the courage to share their stories with me for each and every Sunday Series. There are many more stories to come, Volume I is just the beginning.

I am forever in debt to each of the people in these stories who revealed themselves to me and then trusted me to write their story and share it with the world. There is no doubt the world thanks you for sharing. You can never know the depths to which you touched my heart with your trust and confidence. It is life-affirming and the bond we have formed through this experience fills my soul with love and a great sense of abundance.

Thank you as well to Debbie, the beautiful mother of my beautiful children, Sophie and Emily. The book is dedicated to all three of you as well. Acknowledgements for you can never go deep enough. Ever.

Thank you to my parents, Bonnie and Robin Brodinsky and my sister Donna, your unconditional love and support throughout my life is a constant source of comfort and inspiration in all that I strive to accomplish.

Thank you to Julie Bender, the first person I turned to say – can you help - Julie was instrumental in helping me choose the 33 stories which make up *The Sunday Series, Volume I,* as well as keeping me organized and on-task. Your assistance was heaven sent.

Thank you to the members of my Mastermind Group – Mark Pallack, Rob Commodari and Pete Kohlasch. My brothers you have changed my life. Don't know where I would be without you and your constant support and accountability.

Thank you to Marlo Higgins, my Chief Inspirational Officer and friend for pushing and prodding and the constant confirmation that people want my gift and what I have to offer. You are magic.

Speaking of believing – thanks to my dear friends Julie Bondroff and Ann Hamilton. During a tumultuous year you have been there every step of the way. You both saved me. I'm not at this moment without you.

Thank you to everyone reading this and everyone who has ever read even one of the stories I have written. Your place in my heart is permanent, unwavering and will travel with my spirit now and forever.

And special thanks to all those who don't and might never believe in me. You are my drive and my inspiration. To be everything to everyone means you are nothing to no one. Thanks for telling me this doesn't matter, it can't be done, why do it at all, why even try, you can't change lives. I love all of you for making me know *without a shadow of a doubt* this is not only possible, it's necessary. Stories are the way we define our lives and all stories need to be told.

This book, ***The Sunday Series Volume I*** and the others to follow are part of *my story*.

Everyone has a story.

Foreword

I was extremely honored when asked by Mark Brodinsky to write the foreword for his next book, *The Sunday Series, Volume I*. I first met Mark through another friend in January of 2012. We had lunch and a great conversation about personal growth. I learned Mark had recently embarked on his journey, reading and studying about personal development. He had this fire in his eyes and a desire in his heart. I could feel his energy and knew instantly we would become friends for a long time to come. We were *kindred spirit*.

In reality though, Mark started on his journey 18 months earlier when he discovered his wife had been diagnosed with breast cancer. In his first book, *It Takes 2*, Marks tells us of the journey he and his family experienced as they battled the beast. Mark included his very private thoughts and feelings throughout the journey and the book became a best-seller on Amazon, sharing a message of hope for anyone who reads it, especially those going through the cancer experience.

Since then, I have met with Mark numerous times and have seen him continue to grow. I know he had an Emmy-Award winning career in local TV, he experienced success in the financial services industry and is currently working with USHEALTH Advisors. He is one of the top selling agents in his business. What I know about Mark is even though he is successful in his work; his passion is in his writing. Mark wants to use his writing, to open hearts and create engagement in life and in business, by inspiring people to become the very best version of themselves.

A few years ago I was meeting with Mark and two other friends, Mark Pallack and Pete Kohlasch, who make up our mastermind group, when Mark revealed to us his plans to interview people and start to do storytelling on his blog. His plan was to share their stories of courage, hope and inspiration. Real people facing real challenges. Here we are today as

Mark has interviewed nearly 150 people and inspired millions more. Mark has a goal to connect with at least a **_billion people_** and inspire those who connect with him to share their hearts and to fulfill their potential. He is well on his way.

Mark has converted those interviews into his next bestselling book. You will be moved to higher levels of love and gratitude, as others share their stories and how they have overcome and persevered. I know Mark carries in his heart the desire to inspire everyone he speaks with. You grow to the extent you're willing to grow, which can be unlimited if the learning never ends.

I have so much gratitude and love for my good friend, Mark Brodinsky, and I know as you read through the stories in this book you will be moved. Mark possesses a tremendous gift for writing and sharing his heart. You will feel his energy, his love, and his ability to help us all become the best version of ourselves.

Congratulations Mark, I'm proud to be part of the billion.

Rob Commodari

Preface

You might ask the question - why tell someone else's story?

My answer to you is simple and direct: why not? You matter!

It's almost as if I can't help it. It's been said that we as people don't have dreams, *the dreams have us.* We are each born with a calling - gifts, talents, abilities, even genius - and if we can find a way to figure out our why and our reason for our existence on this planet, then it's time to get going. You can't stop and hold time. The time to share is now.

Part of my gift you currently hold in your hands, or in its digital format on your device. However we have arrived at this introduction let me say, 'hello and welcome'. I am honored you have chosen to invest your time in reading these stories. It's great to meet you and although you will get to know me through my story-telling, we might just meet on a more personal level one day – who knows, I could be telling your story next.

Why not?

For this is the way we define our lives, through the stories we tell. The stories in my Sunday Series are woven together by a common thread – they are all personal tales of courage, hope, or inspiration.

None of us are getting out of this life alive – so we might as well share what we are experiencing, or what we've been through, so that others along our journey can learn… if they can overcome, so can we. If they can do what they are born to do, so can we. If they can love that much – so can we.

Life's about love.

As you will learn through the stories in this very first volume of The Sunday Series you've got to love yourself enough to persevere and love others so much there's nothing you wouldn't do to help see them through. From a young man and his family facing a terminal illness, to a woman living her dream in her house of children, to a man coming back from the brink of death after an accident that left him completely broken – these are the stories that make us stop and think – this is LIFE – we must live through our fears and our victories with equal intensity. Pain is inevitable, suffering is optional.

Or in the words of Les Brown, one of my favorite motivational speakers of all time, "no matter how bad it is, or how bad it gets, I am going to make it. Whatever you are experiencing, it has not come to say, it has come to pass."

Thank you for passing through. I hope once you leave this collection of stories you are inspired by the journey of these people's lives. Ordinary people do extraordinary things every single day. And we are just getting started… work on The Sunday Series Volume II is already underway – the journey continues.

Until next time thanks for taking the time,

Mark

Important Note from The Author

The stories contained in The Sunday Series Volume I are **the original stories in their entirety** written between October 2013 and December 2014. They stand alone in their truth at the moment they were told to me and shared with the world. It is virtually impossible to update each and every story because of the impact on the continuity and core of the original message.

Some updates are included, especially for anyone in any of the stories who are no longer with us. But otherwise the stories are as pure and authentic as the day they were written.

So please understand that while life may have changed over these past three or four years for some of The Sunday Series subjects, as it inevitably does for so many of us, I ask you to accept the stories as they were in the moment.

Courageous. Hopeful. Inspiring.

Now… let's begin.

Introduction

It's the people you meet along the way in your journey that make life so rich. Everyone has a story, even if they think they don't. Everyone is going through, or has gone through something, be it good, bad or somewhere in between.

The process to create *The Sunday Series* is as simple, as it is compelling once it has become the finished product. I interview someone for 60 minutes, usually on the phone, or on an online chat – I take notes and sometimes record the audio portion. I then let the details of their lives marinate inside my heart and soul for about 24-48 hours, I sit down to write and publish… usually all on the same day. An early morning wake-up on Sunday, a quick prayer to bring out the muse, a cup of coffee to jumpstart my brain and I'm on my way.

The stories are shared on the blog, www.markbrodinsky.com, and on all corners of social media, bringing attention to and engagement through these stories of ordinary people overcoming sometimes extraordinary odds. These people fuel me and add light to my life, I hope they do for you as well.

Before we get going, two quotes which I believe define the *reason* for *The Sunday Series* stories to exist and the reason as to why I am the vessel to share these amazing tales.

> *"Listen to your life. See it for the fathomless mystery that it is. Touch, taste, smell our way to the holy and hidden heart of it because in the last analysis all moments are key moments, and life itself is grace."*

> – Frederick Buechner

"In your life's journey, there will be excitement and fulfillment, boredom and routine, and even the occasional train wreck. But when you have picked a dream that is bigger than you personally, that truly reflects the ideals that you cherish, and that can positively affect others, then you will always have another reason for carrying on."

–Pamela Melroy

And now, *The Sunday Series with Mark Brodinsky. Real Stories of Courage, Hope & Inspiration, Volume I.*

The Sunday Series Begins: It's Just About... Life.

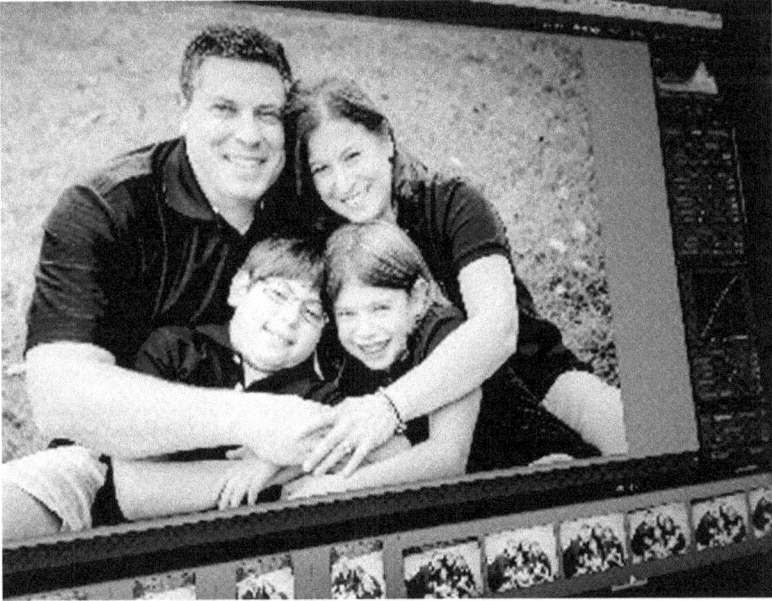

Mark took my words and made them his, as he so lovingly told our Ian's story. Mark has a way of getting your words onto paper with just the right touch. Seeing Ian's story in print, knowing his story was being shared with others made me proud. I was proud to work with Mark, knowing that he would touch others with his new series.

–Marci Scher

I begin a new chapter with the blog today, as I continue with the mission: to become more, by helping others to do the same. In essence, my goal is to touch other people's lives, one word at a time. Beginning this week, it's the **Sunday Series**, something I will make an honest attempt to do every Sunday morning, to tell the world about **you**, to share **your** story.

The stories I am looking to share are those of tremendous courage, hope, inspiration, education and joy. In other words, those people who face great challenges yet find a way to overcome. Those who lead a path we all can aspire to follow. Those who have a way of lifting us up when we're down, AND those who are living the dream, meaning from my point of view, they are doing exactly what they were born to do and have found a way to affect other people. They have been born, and now they know WHY. We can learn great lessons from all of the above.

The first ever in this Sunday Series: Ian's Story.

His name is Ian Scher. He is the son of Marci and Brian Scher, the twin sister of Becca Scher and for most of the ten years of his life...Ian has struggled. Struggled to move, struggled to breathe, struggled to survive. His family has done the same, because every moment of Ian's discomfort steals a piece of their heart.

Ian has a rare motor neuron disease, a mutation of the VRK-1 gene, a degenerative muscular condition. Marci says it is best described as a child's form of ALS. The bottom line...it's a terminal illness. Those are tough words to think, tougher to write, unimaginable to speak out loud, but somehow Marci is able to harness the will to do so. She can say the words out loud because Marci and Brian have accepted the inevitable. Now it's up to them to make Ian's journey as *meaningful* as possible.

Currently, Ian has round-the-clock care, whether it be Marci and Brian, or the daily nurse who comes to the home, (minus the weekend days). Ian has no movement at all, he needs someone nearby in case he wants or needs something and especially if he should experience respiratory distress, (he has a trach and a ventilator, which since coming home from the hospital, have basically saved his life.) Ian can tell you what he needs you to do for him, his parents and his sister have become Ian's hands, arms and legs. But Ian's voice is growing weak and communication has become a challenge.

Ian attends a half-day of school (Chatsworth Elementary) and then he is tutored in math at home a few times a week. He is part of the Gilchrist Kids Palliative Care program, more like hospice-at-home. Home is where the heart is, and Marci, Brian and Becca want him to be there.

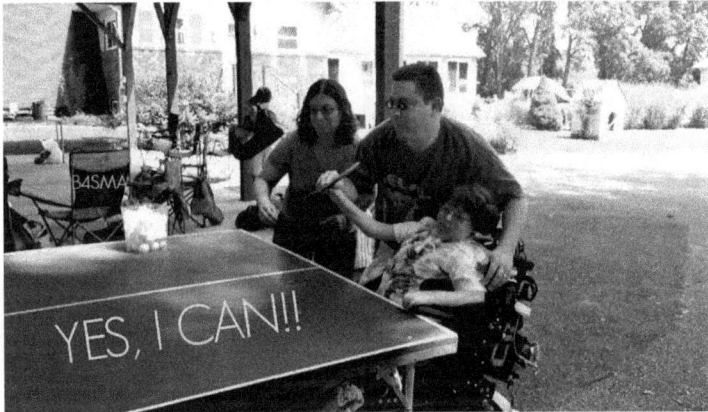

In light of the darkness, there have been moments of wonder: Ian throwing out the first pitch at the Orioles game at Camden Yards this past August, Ian going to sleep away camp this summer for 13 days at Camp Simcha Special. And a few years ago, through the Make-a-Wish Foundation, Ian getting to go to Orlando to meet Spiderman. I would say the honor belonged to Spiderman, since the real superhero was the one who came to see him!

There has been heroism in the Scher's struggle to learn what is wrong with Ian. For most of his life, no one could figure it out. But the Scher's were not giving up. It wasn't until a test, Whole Exome Sequencing, which became commercially available a short time ago, that the family finally could learn the truth. Blood was drawn in March of last year, and by July of 2012, the Scher's had their answer. Ian had the VRK-1 gene mutation, *only one of six people in the world known to have the disease.* Marci and Brian are carriers. The chances of this happening are astronomical. The consequences... devastating.

But Marci told me a big moment in this journey was finding out why. She said, "having diagnosis was a huge weight lifted off of us. A huge loss would have been him passing away and not knowing what it was that caused it." So now there are the day-to-day challenges of Ian's care, but Marci says it's much more than that, "I still remember Ian walking and running around. It's hard seeing other boys doing things I know he wants to be able to do. But maybe the biggest challenge for Marci is, as she says, "in my own mind, imagining what life will be like after. Knowing I can't fix this."

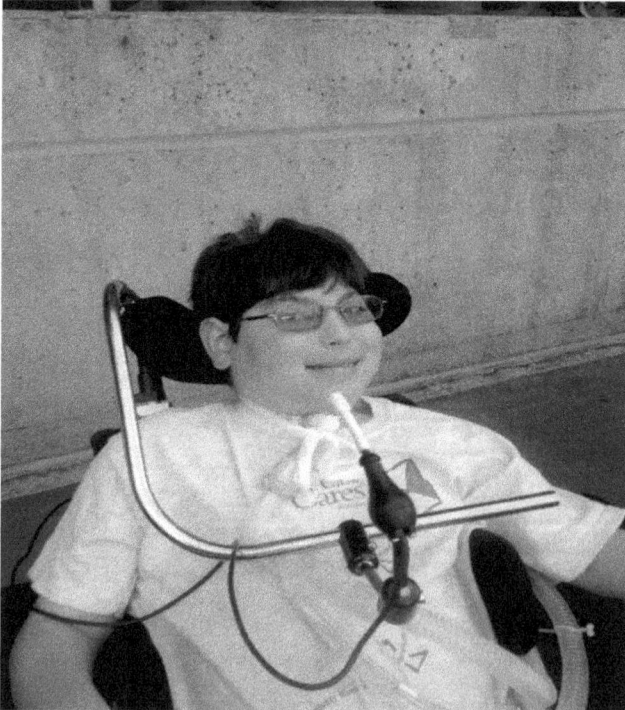

No one can fix it. And this is the reason I chose to tell Ian's story as the first of the Sunday Series for this blog. Take a good look at the Scher family, facing life's greatest loss, and watching it happen in slow motion. But each day they find a way to make every moment count, to give Ian every chance to live as normal an existence as possible, to make sure he gets to experience his share of this world, so he can touch others and have them transformed by him... no matter how much time is left.

Yes, the Scher family is redefining what it means to be courageous, determined and devoted.

Marci says she wants the message of this story to be about education. She wants others to know this gene mutation is out there, so they don't face the same nine-year struggle her family did, trying to find out what was wrong with their child. But whether Marci, Brian and Becca admit it or not, their message goes so much deeper. It's not easy to find the right words when facing the prospect of losing a child, but you need not look far, it's the title of Marci's own journal she is keeping during this journey:

Treasure yesterday. Dream of tomorrow. Live for today.

Thanks Marci we will. And, we will pray for a miracle.

(Update: This story, unfortunately, ended as the Scher family expected. Ian passed away on September 15, 2016. A true superhero to the very end, the world is a far better place because Ian came this way. If you are inspired by Ian's story and wish to honor his life, you can make a donation to: Gilchrist Kids, 11311 McCormick Road, Suite 359, Hunt Valley, Md 21030)

Until next time, thanks for taking the time.

The Sunday Series: Soul Purpose

No one else will ever know the strength of my love for you. After all, you're the only one who knows what my heart sounds like from the inside.

—A quote from any Mother

As a single mother by choice, I believe it is important to share my journey in becoming a mother. It was a hard road with enormous support from other single mothers by choice across the country. Although Mark probably doesn't realize it, he has given me an amazing gift. My journey to be Zoe's mother will forever be documented and is not only a gift for me, but in time she will cherish it as much as I do.

—Traci Kodeck

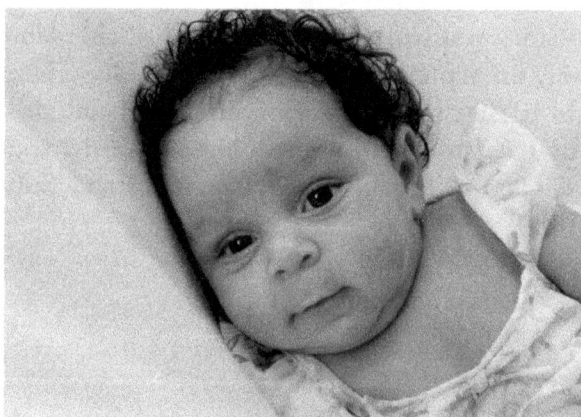

Traci Kodeck yearned to feel that love. She always wanted to be a Mom. But by the time she neared her 39th birthday, the right man had still not come along to help make Traci's dream come true. Or maybe he had, but the right man to Traci was someone who wanted to have children and her last relationship ended for just that reason. No kids, no marriage, no deal. Time to move on.

On a trip to Utah to celebrate her 39th birthday with a good friend, Traci made the decision to go it alone. The desire was too strong, and in human hours, months and years, the clock was ticking. The right man was nowhere in sight. So Traci decided to experience life's greatest miracle on her own and become a single mother. What she didn't know at the time…God had other plans.

As she began her journey, an immediate roadblock surfaced, Traci's doctor ran some tests to check for any structural damage, turns out there was an abnormality in the uterus. A laparoscopic surgery was scheduled for September of 2010 and the issue was corrected. By November of that year, Traci took her first steps toward motherhood by purchasing sperm, and having an insemination.

Her first try was unsuccessful. No go, no pregnancy. Time to get ready for round two.

Even the average woman has only about a 20% chance of actually getting pregnant during each cycle. But for Traci, her second time around she beat the odds. The insemination worked, she was pregnant, but it was short lived. At ten weeks in, Traci had a miscarriage. As anyone who has ever experienced one knows miscarriages are common, but it was still disappointing. Don't forget Traci was making this journey alone. She said her family and friends were incredibly supportive, but it was her dream, her desire, her destiny and she wanted it more than anything else.

A third try, then a fourth, but with no success. But on the fifth insemination, it took hold and Traci was pregnant again. It was pure joy that lasted less than two months. At seven weeks the baby's heart stopped beating. The summer of 2011 was now one of discontent and disappointment. In the midst of all these attempts, the doctors, including a high risk OB, were busy running all sorts of tests. One theory for all the trouble was possible chromosomal conflict. But nothing conclusive. The only thing anyone knew for sure, Traci's dream was on hold again, but her desire for that feeling of unconditional love kept her fight going. Sometimes to witness a miracle you need a little help along the way.

During this period Traci found a place of refuge, reflection and community, (http://www.singlemothersbychoice.org/). There she could communicate with others going through the same challenges, setbacks and stories of success, which kept her inspired. She needed it, especially after her sixth and seventh tries were still unsuccessful. Pregnancy seemed like a distant dream and one that was drifting further and further away.

Trying?

But as Traci soon discovered, the global community created by the internet might just be the greatest single invention in recorded history to bring humans together. Traci was flying solo, but was always just one click away from a friend fighting for the same dream, and if lucky, soaring high and living that dream as well.

Mothering?

By her eighth attempt at pregnancy, a long-time friend had come to Traci's rescue, offering to be a sperm donor. But the end result was the same...a miscarriage. Another try, now number nine, ended the same as all the others. The road to a dream was getting rough, but sometimes pursuit of that dream and failure after failure leads you to look for another path, a different light, a new way. Through the single mother online support group, Traci found the Colorado Center for Reproductive Medicine (CCRM). A phone consult, a plane ride out west, meetings with social workers, financial counselors and a complete range of new testing and finally the doctors were ready for a recommendation: IVF with genetic testing. This time the process would start outside Traci's body – in a petri dish in Denver – and if the embryo was healthy it would then be placed inside, for Traci to carry the baby to term.

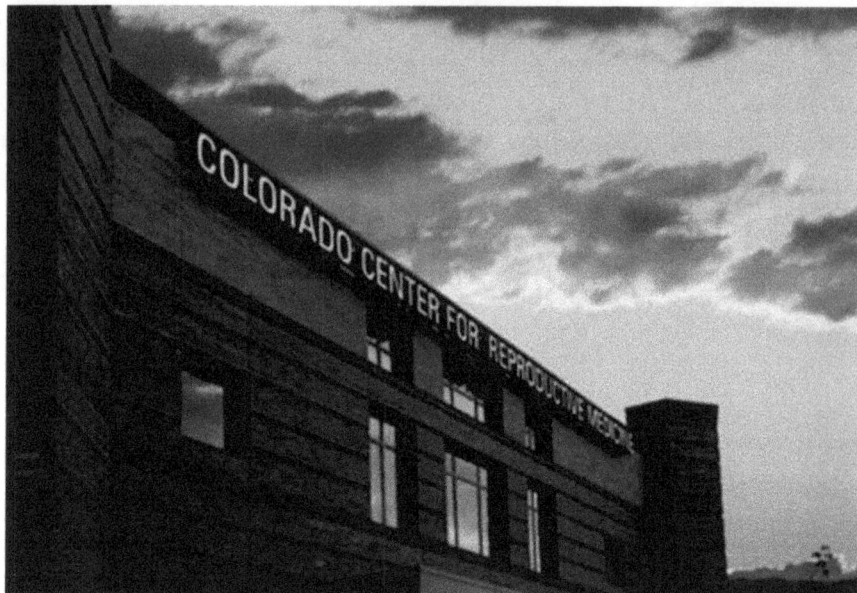

The process was a success, six embryos were created, and each one had a cell removed for genetic testing. Two weeks after those tests began, the doctors called. Only one of the six embryos was healthy, the other five had chromosomal abnormalities. Traci's chances were down to a single embryo. If this didn't work, she was out of options AND out of money. Her best and only chance was this single embryo, a $30,000 roll of the dice. There were no more dollars for another go-round and after nine other tries if Traci had to call it quits, who could blame her. She had given it everything she had, her time, her money, her heart. If this was to be her higher calling, then this was her moment.

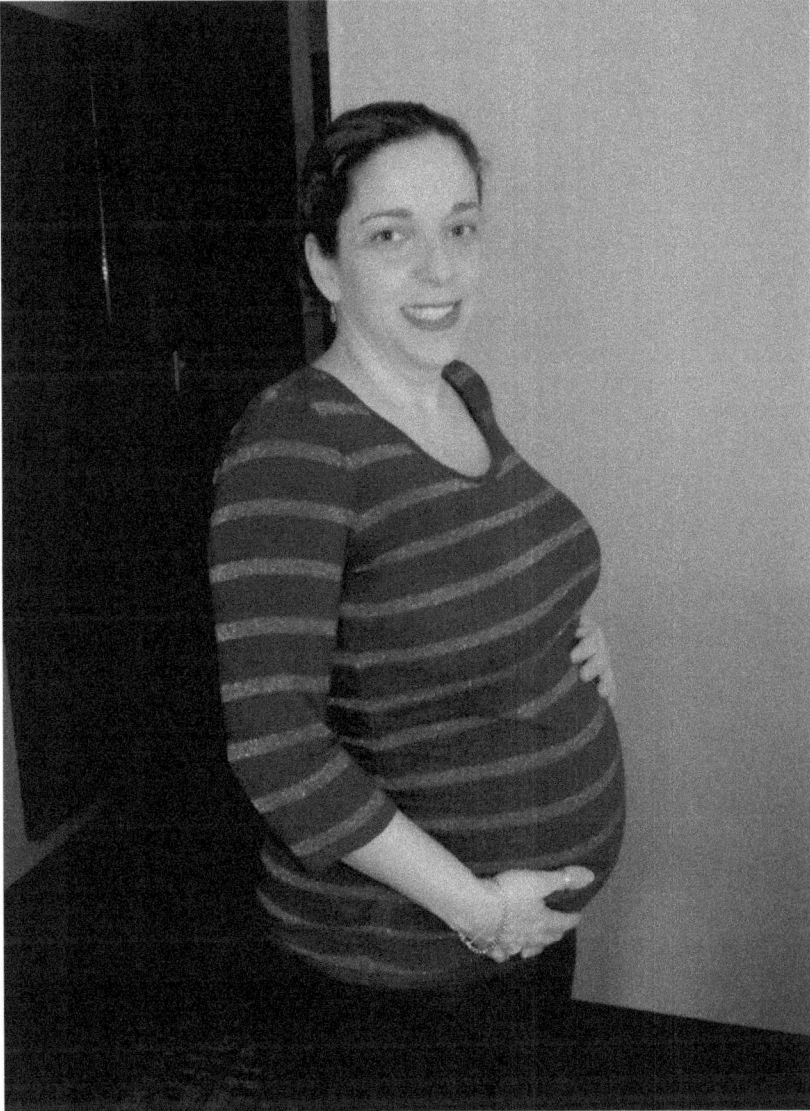

August 24th, 2012, Traci flew back to Denver for the frozen embryo transfer. Two weeks later and now back home, Traci had confirmation... she was pregnant. Her local OB kept close watch, checkups every two weeks, and this time she made it to the end of the first trimester. And because of the genetic testing, Traci got some bonus news, the doctors could tell her the baby's sex, Traci now knew she was having a girl. She was three months in now; her longest pregnancy to date.

The days passed. Fall turned to Winter. Winter turned to Spring. It was almost time.

If you want to learn what humility is, create life. If you want to know what love is, hold a child in your arms. If you want to know what a miracle is, talk to Traci. She knows and she can tell you the moment: May 6th, 2013, 11:37AM. She can tell you the size of that miracle, seven pounds, three ounces. And she can tell you the name of that miracle: Zola.

In all of human history, there is no greater gift than that of life. To hold a child, your child, and to feel two hearts beat as one. Traci Kodeck made the choice and took that journey alone. She fought for and found her soul purpose.

And now Traci will never be alone again.

Until next time, thanks for taking the time.

The Sunday Series: Remembering Jerry G.

"He could meet someone waiting in line and just start up a conversation and be best friends by the time they got to the cash register."

–Harold Deutsch

"You could see his soul in his eyes... and it was a good one"

–Barry Grosshandler

There are people you meet in life who touch you and then there are people who leave an indelible mark on your soul. I'm not going to pretend today's Sunday Series isn't personal, it is. It's still someone else's story, but the man can no longer speak for himself he's gone. Today is the anniversary of his death. I'm going to tell his story through the eyes, words and hearts of those who knew him best; the man I was lucky enough to call Dad.

The smile. That smile. His smile.

Talk to almost anyone who met or knew Jerry Gross and that is what they will tell you about him, the man was always smiling and it was infectious. In his later years, he had a ton of crows feet and little slits for eyes, no doubt from all the years of smiling. But it wasn't always like that.

Jerry was born to Bernice and Dave on December 7th, 1944 and the early years, first in Brooklyn, New York and then in Baltimore, were not easy ones for Jerry. His father was a disciplinarian, Jerry was a bit mischievous and the two found it hard to mesh. Dave was tough on his boy and Jerry's self-confidence and school work suffered because of it. The battle of wills continued until Jerry's late teens, but then things started to change and for only one reason: Sharon.

Jerry met Sharon at Forest Park High School. He was 17, Sharon was 15. Jerry got word Sharon had just broken up with her boyfriend. His self-confidence still shaky, he had someone else call her to see if she would go out with him. She said yes and it soon became another reason for Jerry to smile. The first date was a trip down to see the local goings-on for the Jerry Lewis Labor Day Telethon...the rest is history. Jerry and Sharon dated for a few years and married September 5th, 1965. The relationship, the marriage, helped warm up Jerry's Dad. Dave liked Sharon, and approved of his son's choice, the relationship between father and son warmed, until Dave's untimely death just after the birth of his first granddaughter Alisa, in 1967.

After working a few different jobs, Jerry found his comfort zone as a salesman in the optical business. It was a perfect fit, because that smile could win accounts. "If he was selling it, they bought it from him, because of him," Sharon says. "They would always buy from him no matter what it was." Jerry's ability to sell earned him a promotion and the opportunity to earn a good living, but it also meant a lot of travel. The travel meant sacrifice and once his daughters Alisa and Debbie were born, it got even tougher.

Jerry's best friend Harold Deutsch explains, "Jerry struggled with traveling to make a living and missing a lot of his family milestones, birthdays, anniversaries... it tore him up quite frankly." Although away from home quite a bit, Jerry did his best to have a normal family life. Barry Grosshandler, Jerry's first cousin and good friend says, "Jerry really strived to build a family life regardless of the negative side of the business and always kept his family first. He (Jerry) always looked at the half-full side of the glass, not the negative side of business or life."

Harold and Barry also echo the same sentiments about Jerry...his special talents which made him a success in business and in life; his smile, his ability to talk to anyone and most importantly, the one trait so many of us struggle to master, the ability to listen. "Jerry was a good listener, a real good listener," says Barry. "He could listen and he would get involved, he could get very emotionally in touch." "Everybody loved him," says Harold. "He could walk into a room with twenty people there, stay for an hour and know half their life's stories. He was very likeable, precarious, great smile. I know everyone who worked with him and in later years when he was in management, everyone who worked for him loved him and were inspired by him."

Jerry's smile provided hope, his words of encouragement and positive outlook gave others inspiration. People wanted to know him, to talk to him, to spend time with him. His sister, Barbara: "His constant smile and crinkly eyes had a warmth to them. He could speak to anyone and make them feel good. He is unforgettable."

His daughters will never forget. I asked Alisa, Jerry's first-born, how he inspired others: "His uncanny ability to know you and make you feel special. That applied not only to his family, though for sure they were his core and most important in his universe, it was anyone and everyone he met. When you spoke to my Dad you were listened to and heard." I posed the same question to Jerry's baby girl, Debbie: "It was his smile and his ability to make you feel good," she said. "I felt safe when he was around."

Jerry was blessed with these two daughters in his life and then four more girls, his grandchildren, Jordan, Sophie, Riley and Emily, whom he completely adored. He was their "Poppy". They changed his life, much like Alisa's birth had done for his own father. Six births in all, and Jerry finally got the chance to witness one of them. He was there in the room, right by Debbie's side, as Emily was born on July 16, 2002. That day, Jerry's smile was a mile wide.

Miracles happen, but sometimes the ones you pray for don't. In June of 2009, Jerry was diagnosed with esophageal cancer, stage 3. He fought long and hard, enduring torturous doses of chemotherapy, radiation, and then in late October of that same year, an all-day surgery to remove the mass. Jerry survived the long operation, but just a few days away from being released from the hospital, there were complications. This time the glass tipped to half-empty, and even with all the life energy Jerry created for others with his love, laughter and goodwill, there wasn't enough left to save him.

On November 3rd, 2009, they turned off the machines and with his family by his side, Jerry died. Just ten days before that, Debbie and I visited with Jerry in the hospital, he had been doing quite well. We had a party to go to that evening, so we stopped in to see him before heading out. Jerry was feeling alright, but then suddenly he wasn't. He got bad chills and had some slight difficulty in breathing. After all he had been through we thought it was just a slight setback. The nurses gave him some oxygen and we figured he would be Ok, so we decided to leave.

As Debbie and I said goodbye to Jerry that evening, we couldn't lean over the bed to hug him, for fear of giving his chemotherapy-ravaged body an infection. So I got as close as I could and we did a fist-bump. He said the same thing he had said to me hundreds of times before, "I love you bud." I said "I love you too, Dad." And then he smiled. I didn't know then it was the last one I would ever see. But it lives on....forever.

Until next time, thanks for taking the time.

The Sunday Series: Flowers for Powers

I think they will learn that life is not all about taking. It's about giving too and they are learning from this experience that if you continue to give back and support your community that only good things will come to you as well. They are doing this so selflessly. They don't expect anything, or are asking for anything in return. They are doing this out of the goodness of their hearts.

–Sherri Thomas

"I know a girl... she puts the color inside of my world."

–Daughters, by John Mayer

I know a couple of girls too, they are 10-year-old Lexi Thomas and Abby Levin, and if you want color in your world and a smile on your face, or the face of someone you love, they're ready. Meet Flowers for Powers.

It all began in May of this year. Abby and Lexi are jumping on the trampoline and see some beautiful flowers. They take them inside and wonder if they could take these flowers to those who are sick, maybe suffering from cancer, or seniors spending their final years in nursing homes, or assisted living centers. Flowers for Powers is born, bringing healing powers and smiles to those who need it the most. Once you focus in on love, it knows no boundaries. Love can come in many forms, in this case it's from the hearts of two girls, bringing beautiful flowers, even more beautiful smiles and trying to bring the same to the faces of others who maybe haven't felt like smiling for quite some time.

The very first stop for the girls was the FutureCare Nursing Home outside of Baltimore. The first recipient, a lady named Ruth. You never forget your first. Since that first bouquet, that first smile, that first good feeling, the girls have brought healing powers to more than a thousand people.

Hospitals, cancer treatment and infusion centers, nursing homes, assisted living centers, and even door-to-door to visit special peoples' homes, like breast cancer survivor Ellen Logwood, or (the late) Ian Scher, who suffered from a rare motor neuron disease.

And let me pause for a moment of synergy that is too powerful to ignore. I started the Sunday Series a few weeks ago with a story about Ian Scher and his inspirational family, (http://markbrodinsky.com/2013/10/13/the-sunday-series-begins-its-just-about-life/), who could know that the same week I wanted to showcase Flowers for Powers, the girls would visit Ian at his home, just days before this blog post. The coincidence is too strong, sometimes you throw a pebble in the water and make a wave, keep this going we're going to have a tsunami, for good.

And speaking of doing good, it's what all of this mean to the girls. Abby says, "I feel good about myself, the people usually thank us and smile and it makes me feel good because I made their day better." Lexi echoes those feelings, "we get excited by their reactions. I feel proud, proud because of what I'm doing, because it's a good thing to do, because we are helping people feel good about themselves, even though they are sick." The girls already have so many special memories of their experiences, every life touched, every smile given, warms their hearts. Lexi says one of her favorite experiences was a woman they met at a cancer center, she started crying when the girls gave her flowers because it was her 10-year anniversary as a cancer survivor. The woman told the girls, "you never know where you are going to meet angels."

Then there was this younger man the girls met getting an infusion at GBMC's cancer center. The first time Abby and Lexi met him, he was warm and welcoming and took pictures with them, even while going through his treatment that day. But when the girls came back for another visit he was asleep during his infusion, so the girls left the flowers next to him while they finished their rounds. Before they left, the same man tracked them down in the parking lot, gave them a hug and told the girls they should have woken him, he wanted to see them because he thought what they were doing is so special and they are changing lives.

Yes, changing lives. And not just the patients, but the girls as well. When you give, you get back a million times over. Abby and Lexi are also transformed by their experience and their moms, who are an integral part of scheduling the visits, helping make arrangements, collecting donations and most importantly, transporting their Flowers for Powers girls to their destination, agree. Lexi's mom, Sherri Thomas: "I think they will learn that life is not all about taking. It's about giving too and they are learning from this experience that if you continue to give back and support your community that only good things will come to you as well. They are doing this so selflessly. They don't expect anything, or are asking for anything in return. They are doing this out of the goodness of their hearts."

Abby's mom, Lisa Levin says she doesn't know where to begin. "Sherri and I look at each other at times and it's unbelievable how (the girls) are affected, yet unaffected. They will approach anybody, they want to help children, they know what the bigger picture is and they get that. It's a wonderful thing." Flowers for Powers also made an appearance at a walk for ALS this year, the same disease which claimed the life of Lisa's mom. Lisa says it was beyond words to see the girls there, to watch them go up to these people give them hugs and bring them flowers.

Flowers for Powers is a big success, so much so that it became necessary to turn it into a non-profit foundation. Sherri says they never thought to do something like a non-profit, but people started donating money early on and it was money they certainly didn't want to keep. All the funds go back to the foundation, to help with things like buying vases, making t-shirts, promotion and even the gasoline used to get the girls from place to place. Most of the flowers are donated as well, from places like Flowers for Fancies, and B' More Organic. So where does Flowers for Powers go from here? Sherri says as long as the girls want to do this, they will. No one is forcing them, they love it. The girls always talk about how good they feel when they leave each place, and she says it's their big grins and sweet voices, along with the flowers, that change the day for a cancer-victim, a senior, or simply someone in need. "You don't find many 10-year-olds who want to do this and spend their weekends doing it as well," says Sherri.

So this labor of love for Lexi Thomas and Abby Levin continues. Flowers for Powers is bringing healing and smiles wherever they go. And if you like what the girls are doing, then do them a favor, head over to their Facebook page and LIKE it as well.

(https://www.facebook.com/pages/
Flowers-for-Powers/285248074943951)

The more we all give, the more colorful this world can be.

Until next time, thanks for taking the time.

The Sunday Series: A Fight to the Finish

Mark Brodinsky shared our family's story with the world for the first time on November 17, 2013. Daron and I were not Caring-Page type folks, so only our close friends really knew what life was like for us. When Mark approached me, I felt it was time for Daron's brain cancer journey to reach a wider audience. Mark listened to our story and then shared it with grace, understanding and empathy. His words touched our family, helped others understand the experience of living with brain cancer, and let potential donors and recipients know about the work of Keep Punching.

Thank you Mark, for your compassion in sharing our message.

–Beth Fisher

Throughout history there have been epic battles fought in the ring: Ali vs Frazier. Leonard vs Hearns. Tyson vs almost anyone in the 1st round. Even the make-believe heavyweight fights we love up on the big screen, including the king of them all, Rocky.

Then there are the epic fights which might take place just around the corner, sometimes in the shadows, without fanfare, but with a much deeper meaning than a simple sporting event. A battle for survival. This is the story of one such fighter, Daron Fisher.

It was August of 2010, Daron, a healthy 43-year-old father of two, suffers a seizure on the train ride back from New York. He was returning from helping with a marketing campaign for MGH advertising. For Daron, the job he loved was about to take a back seat to a bigger challenge; tests showed a small mass inside his brain, a tumor. Daron's wife Beth, remembers the time well. She recalls the need for immediate surgery and then test after test after test.

Weeks passed and then what Beth describes as an "insane sick feeling," when the doctor read the results: brain cancer, specifically a glioblastoma, prognosis on survival with treatment...about 15 months. The good news, the specialists said the tumor was small, about the size of a jelly bean and when they removed it they got it "all." Except when it comes to the "C" word, getting it all doesn't mean it's all over. A tumor in the brain is like a pile of sand, you can remove it, but there may be a grain or two that shakes loose. Despite Daron's incredibly positive attitude, healthy living, better diet, increased exercise and the like... the smallest of possibilities, that tiny shadow of a doubt, that grain of sand, re-surfaced. The tumor returned.

The week of Thanksgiving 2011, Daron was back in surgery, but this time the tumor was too close to a blood vessel in the brain and the doctors couldn't get it "all." Time was no longer on Daron's side. Throughout the ordeal, Beth and Daron chose to keep the diagnosis a secret from their young children, Emory and Alana. They didn't want to burden their kids with worry, fear, sadness and the realization that their father and the life they had come to know would never be the same. So for the Fisher kids, life went on pretty much uninterrupted. Daron still coached Emory's baseball games, went to Alana's gymnastic practices and the family did what families do best when love is at its core... spend time together, enjoying this journey we call life, made all the more fulfilling when you share it with the people who share your heart.

In the meantime, Daron went on secret doctor appointments, endured chemotherapy and radiation. He sought out aggressive treatment through the National Cancer Institute, and Beth and Daron were aided and supported by a great friend and advocate, Ellen Hakim. But despite everyone's best efforts and a number of alternative therapies, by October of 2012 things were getting worse, not better. To try a device called Novacure, electromagnetic headgear designed at "zapping" the brain cancer, Daron would have to shave his head...*now* the kids needed to know.

Beth remembers she had never used the "C" word, but now there was no choice. Beth says telling their children was not, as she remembers the "most awful thing ever." "I imposed expectations that didn't surface," says Beth. And her children, now ages 8 and 11, took the news in stride, proving their resilience, yet at the same time shielded by a lack of life experience to truly comprehend the outcome, one which, unless there was a miracle, would one day leave them without their "Daddy."

As time ticked away, the cancer continued to take its toll and the calendar turned to 2013. In January, the illness was robbing Daron of his strength and he was forced to go on disability. Even worse, he could no longer do one of the things he adored...play guitar. It was devastating to Daron, but his will would not be defeated. Daron started telling Beth stories, including one from years ago in which his uncle, a media promoter, had secured a media kit from the movie Rocky II and had given it to Daron and his brother. The poster, signed by Sylvester Stallone himself, reads "Keep Punching." An idea was born.

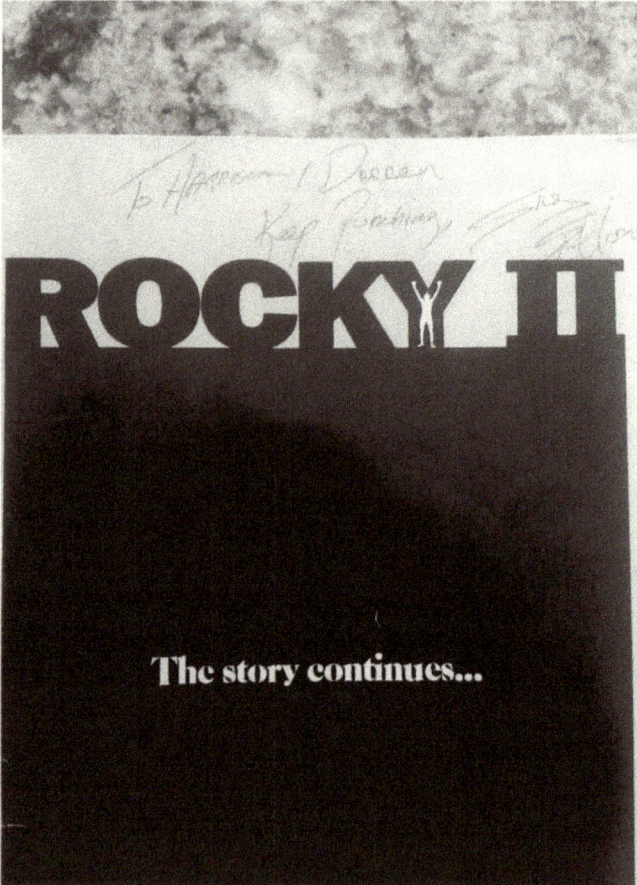

Daron and Beth wanted to find a way to give back. There was a special researcher, Dr. Fabio Iwamoto, whom they met at the National Cancer Institute. Dr. Iwamoto had gone above and beyond, following their progress, checking in with late night phone calls, showing care and compassion. Beth and Daron thought how great would it be if they could find a way to raise money to fund Dr. Iwamoto's research at Columbia University in New York. A small idea became a big hit and Keep Punching, with a big hand from Beth's good friend Jen Johnson, orchestrated a major fundraiser on March 23rd of 2013. More than 225 people attended the event at Frazier's Restaurant and Bar in Hampden, Maryland... even Daron was able to make it, and so together a village of love and support raised $20,000. They say it takes a village to raise a child, it takes that same village when a family is in pain, providing love and support so desperately needed to see them through.

Dr. Carroll, Dr. Iwamoto and the Keep Punching Team

Daron Writing $20,000 Check for Columbia University

Keep Punching was a huge success (www.keeppunching.org). And there was another milestone to come. The Fisher family and the Hakim family traveled to Philadelphia in the early spring of 2013. If you're going to keep punching, it means you must be fighting.... and because of Daron's hard work and intensive therapy, he was able to accomplish a dream. Daron climbed the "Rocky" steps, and for a moment make-believe became reality. For a moment, the "C" word changed from cancer to congratulations. For a moment, Daron got the chance to taste victory, a delicacy not so prevalent in the 2-1/2 years since his life had changed forever. And Daron was already beating the odds. The doctors said 15 months, by this time, Daron had doubled down.

Beth met Daron back in 1996, both of them worked at TBC advertising agency in Baltimore. They were wed in 1999, and danced their first dance to More Today than Yesterday…"I love you more today than yesterday, but not as much as tomorrow"…lyrics that launched Beth and Daron's lives together and still ring true today. As the years moved forward, Daron and Beth brought two children into the world, and created layer upon layer of memories. But on August 9th, 2013, their lives together became just that… as Daron passed away, with his family by his side, succumbing to the brain cancer which three years earlier surfaced on the train tracks heading home.

When someone you love becomes a memory, that memory becomes a treasure. Inside all of us are hidden treasures. The greatest challenge in life is not to die with that treasure hidden inside you. Daron Fisher brought his to the surface for all the world to see, as a loving husband and a devoted father. He displayed great wit, especially in his work as a talented copywriter. Just last month Daron was honored posthumously with a Lifetime Achievement Award by the American Advertising Foundation. But his greatest rewards were his family and friends. Beth says, "everyone who knew Daron and knew his wit and his kindness...everybody loved him, no one could say a bad word about him. He was caring and loving. I want Daron to be remembered for who he was and not for who he became." It was the cancer that robbed Daron of his freedom of movement, and his ability to think with clarity, but not his spirit. His brain was ravaged by the beast, but his heart still full with the more than forty years of the love he gave and received.

A fighter to the end Daron Fisher went the distance. He gave it all he had. Daron kept punching and fought more rounds than any scorecard could ever record, and in the end he went down for the count. But there's a huge difference between losing a fight in the ring and the one outside the ropes. For Beth, for Emory, for Alana, for all the family and friends who Daron touched and who gave that love right back...that village knows another champion.

Until next time, thanks for taking the time.

The Sunday Series: TLC

Mark went out in a limb when he heard about my foundation, Touching Lives With Comfort. He took the chance to learn about the mission of my foundation and what drove me to create such a foundation, and then he shared it with the world. Mark cares deeply about people and the stories that inspire change and good in people.

I've been following Mark and his Sunday Series, stories of inspiration for a couple of years now, and I've learned so much from each story; stories of hope, inspiration, love and change. I've taken what I've learned and shared it with others. I know that my story about what lead me to create my foundation has touched others and has helped spread the word about TLC. Mark has an exquisite way with writing and expressing what the storyteller is trying to convey. You will not be disappointed with Mark's writing and stories of inspiration - stories that will leave an impression on your heart forever."

–Michele McFarland

"They know me in a way no one ever has. They open me to things I never knew existed. They drive me to insanity and push me to my depths. They are the beat of my heart, the pulse of my veins, and the energy in my soul. They are my kids."

–A quote from any parent who loves a child.

There may be no greater sense of satisfaction, no better feeling of inner gratitude, than to touch the heart of a child. The McFarland family knows this feeling well. For the past several years they have touched thousands of young hearts, with an idea as cool as the other side of the pillow...because it is one.

In fact, it was 6-year-old Chloe McFarland's pillow pet, the one she got as a gift a few years ago, at the tender age of six, which gave birth to an idea.

Chloe loved that first pillow pet and wondered if other children might also enjoy the chance to share the same joy, especially those who don't have much joy this time of year, those who are very sick, spending their holidays in the hospital. Maybe another child might like to have a soft, cuddly pet to call their own. Sometimes, maybe most times, all it takes is a simple, noble idea to start a chain of events. This idea now lives as the Touching Lives with Comfort Foundation, TLC for short.

Back in 2010, long on an idea but short on time to implement it, Chloe's mom Michele, a human resources worker at the Baltimore County Department of Social Services, got to work. Understand Michele has organized holiday toy drives before, collecting and donating toys to the same government facility where she is employed. And the McFarland family– Michele, her husband Brian, daughter Chloe and son Liam, had volunteered their time before at cancer foundations and for other causes.

Fortunately for the critically ill children and their parents, the McFarland family was no stranger to giving and Michele especially knows how to get things accomplished. Talk to her for even a few minutes and you know she's a woman with a huge heart and a big plan in place to share it.

Michele first contacted Johns Hopkins Hospital in Baltimore about the idea and at the time the heads of the hospital hadn't even heard of a pillow pet. After doing some checking the hospital administrators called Michele back. They loved the idea, said they would love to participate and, oh, by the way, they would need 200 pillows.

Put a challenge in front of Michele McFarland and her family and watch them respond. Michele got to work telling friends and family about what she and her family wanted to accomplish. She sent e-mails asking for others to donate the pillow pets, or to donate the dough, ($20 at the time), to be able to secure 200 pillow pets in time for Christmas. She contacted CJ products, the maker of the furry friends, told them what she was doing and was thrilled to learn the company was willing to help; they would sell the pillow pets to her at cost. Now the wheels were really in motion.

Between donations of pillow pets delivered right to the McFarland's home, in a big, over-sized drop-off box right on their porch, cash donations and the help of CJ products, the McFarland's collected 250 pets and delivered them to the Johns Hopkins Children's Center that year. The hospital asked Santa to help deliver the pets to the sick children who now had the benefit of a physical and emotional security blanket, a distraction from the stress of surgeries, tests and rigors of recovery, if they're lucky enough to get that far.

The Very First Pillow Pet Delivery!

When a child is sick, everything matters and these small gestures made a huge difference. Not only was this act of giving unique, originating from the innocent, yet grand idea of another child, but the McFarland's were doing it without ever getting to see the end results of their generosity. Because of the risk of germs and infection, the McFarland's could not enter the hospital rooms, instead they gave the pillow pets to the nurses, child life specialists and social workers to handle and then transfer them to Santa for special delivery. It was through e-mails, letters and phone calls the McFarland's learned of their success. "I've always been someone who cares for other people," says Michele. "Knowing we can do something, even though we don't get to see it, to help kids get through uncomfortable times, makes me feel like I'm doing something worthwhile."

Chloe, now 10, echoes her mom's sentiments, "I always wanted to do something to help and I just get really happy doing something for the kids, not just the kids, but for the world itself."

The Hopkins experiment was such a huge success, the McFarland's created a non-profit, (the name of the foundation coming from one of Michele's Facebook friends), and now entering its fourth year, Touching Lives with Comfort is doing it again this holiday season. Since the first delivery, the foundation has delivered about 4,000 pillow pets and collected close to $20,000 in donations. Pillow pets have now found homes in the arms of children at dozens of hospitals and other facilities, like the Ronald McDonald House of Baltimore. The House has a tag line which is in perfect synergy with the mission of TLC..."life will take them many places, we just never expect the journey will lead them here." Who doesn't want to find a way to help a sick child? The McFarland family, friends, co-workers and now dozens of volunteers, are finding a way.

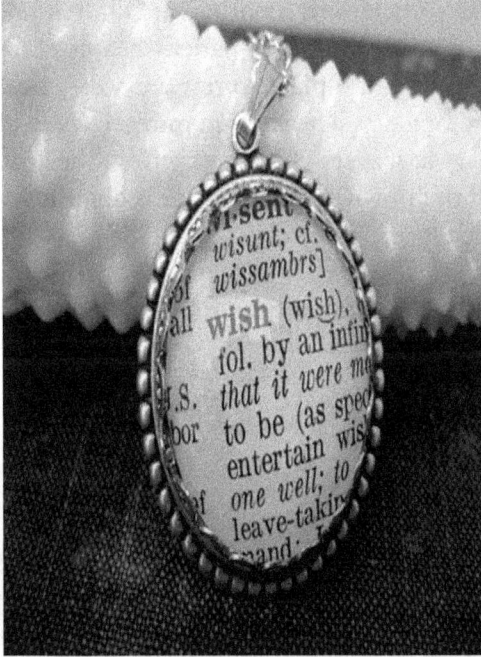

The program has even expanded to include something called "Kapes for Kids," providing superhero capes to lift children's spirits, and give them the super powers to battle their illness. And another popular program, "Remembering Moms" necklaces with messages of inspiration, which are given as Mother's Day gifts to the courageous moms who fight every step of the way, and feel every ounce of pain right along with their children. Doing something for the parents is the extended vision Michele has for the foundation, "I would really like to provide some more types of services to parents, like Yoga classes and massages, services that might be beneficial, to relieve stress and lift spirits."

TLC recently held a fundraiser at the Phoenix Restaurant in Ellicott City, raising more than $5,000 for the cause. It's dollars and donations of time, which are in greatest demand. Each and every pillow pet which is purchased, or donated, is then individually tagged with information about TLC and boxed up, twelve at a time, to be delivered to the hospitals and facilities. The more people who can help, tag, box and deliver, the better. You can e-mail touchingliveswithcomfort@gmail.com or visit their Facebook page, and either send a message or post your request to help.

The National Center for Health reports that children under the age of 18 account for more than 2 million in-patient hospital stays each year. We all know a pillow represents a place to rest our weary heads after the stress and challenges of a long day. The stressed mind of a sick child needs a little extra love as well. What if every child, weary from their journey, could have a pillow pet to call their own? The challenge is big, the McFarland family's heart might just be bigger.

I'm sure every child whose life has been touched with comfort would surely agree.

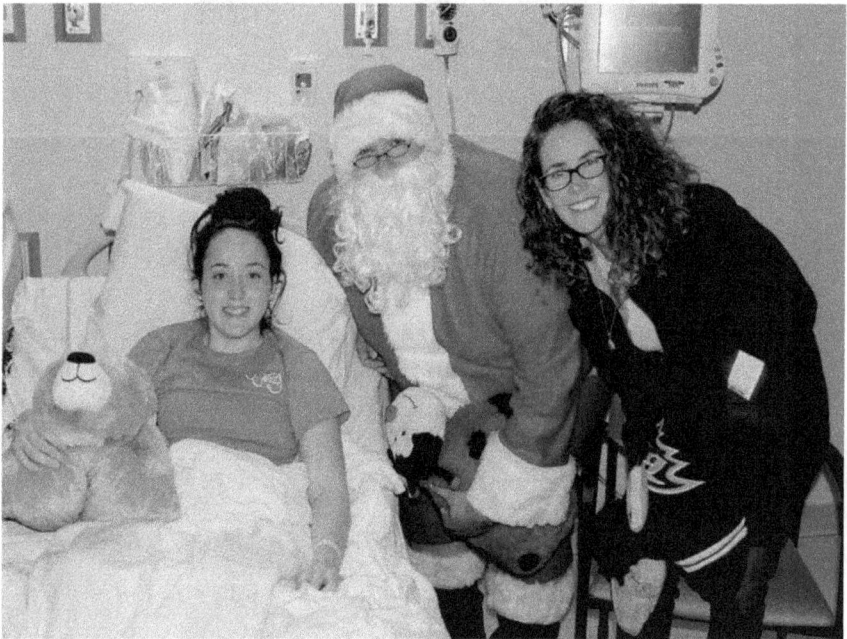

Until next time, thanks for taking the time.

The Sunday Series: Sandy & The House That Love Built

To love, to give, to serve." This is Mark Brodinsky's mantra and he lives it every day. Mark uses his beautiful gift of storytelling to share inspiration, hope, motivation and encouragement around the world. He does this by telling the stories of everyday people who are doing their best to make a difference on this planet, to live a life of significance. Some in big ways, some in small ways but all in the name of love and service. I was honored to be one of Mark's earliest profiles, and humbled that he told my story.

–Sandy Pagnotti

"There is no doubt I was born to do it. This may sound corny, but literally, for most of my adult life, I always had this voice in my head, like what is it? I know there is something, what is it? I kept thinking it was when I had my family, my house of children. But still, what is it? What am I supposed to be doing? Then I got this job, and I heard the voice say this is your house of children and since I took this job here I have total clarity of purpose. I no longer have the question, what is it I am supposed to be doing. I found it...or it found me."

Wow. We are two months into the Sunday Series and the quote above is one of the best answers I have been given so far. It comes from one of the most outstanding women you will ever meet. And I'm not alone in that point of view, she is the best of the best, a Circle of Excellence Inductee into the Top 100 Women of Maryland. You'd be hard pressed to find a more compassionate, dedicated servant to her purpose, the President and CEO of the Ronald McDonald House Charities of Baltimore, Sandy Pagnotti.

Sandy says not only has she found her place, but it's ironic she is working at a place with McDonald's in its title, since when she was in college, she actually spent three summers packing cups on the McDonald's Restaurant line at the Maryland Cup Factory. Who knew then that the college co-ed would one day be the leader of a McDonald's legacy, as part of one of the world's most respected philanthropic organizations, The Ronald McDonald House.

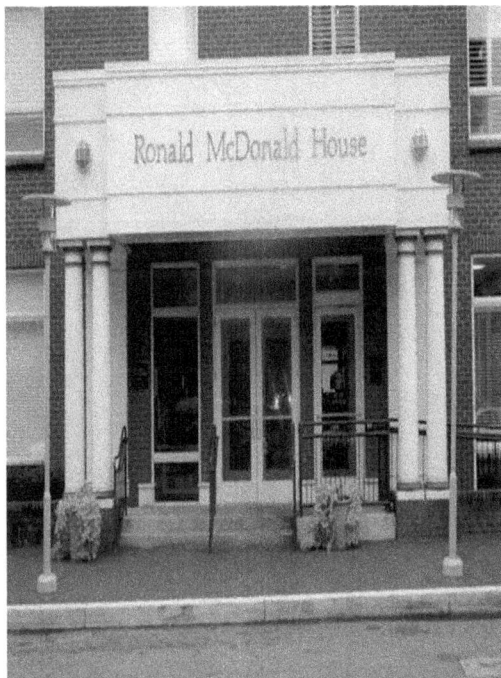

A quick pause here to explain for some who don't know about the House and it's mission. I serve on the Board of Directors for RMH, and I meet people all the time who don't have a clear idea of what the Ronald McDonald House is all about. First the official explanation, then I will give you Sandy's, as only she can describe it.

From the website, www.rmhcbaltimore.org: Ronald McDonald House *Charities of Baltimore provides a home away from home for seriously ill children and their families, and helps to fund programs in the local area that directly improve the well-being of children.*

Now from Sandy: "The way I describe it, it's the Four Seasons Hotel meets Disney meets grandma's house. It's five-star service, a focus on magic and kids and love, warmth and nurturing. Sandy says the experience she wants is for families who are going through one of the toughest experiences of their lives to walk into Ronald McDonald House and feel a huge sense of relief, that they will be catered to and well-cared for, a huge weight lifted off their shoulders and for the kids to walk in and say, "Wow!"

Since the fall of 2010, when Sandy took over as head of the House, (at least half-a-dozen people told her about the job as soon as it became available that summer), she and her team have been laser-focused on living up to the mission. And it's not an easy mission to accomplish. The families of these children are at the end of their ropes, most of the children are being treated at, or even confined to nearby hospitals as they battle illnesses or deal with life-long disabilities. It's stressful and overwhelming for the families and their children and it's the sole purpose for Sandy and her dedicated team to focus and do the best they can to bring what Sandy describes as, "joy to their journey."

"I get asked all the time, isn't your job sad?" says Sandy. "Not if we can help it, it's not. Some days yes, I am overwhelmed by the tragedy of what can go on here, but I am also overwhelmed by the volunteers and community and support. Some days you can't get over the generosity and kindness of what people do for us. There are days I leave and sit in my car thinking, *"people are so good, people are so good."*

Sandy says her favorite part of the job is that the House and staff offer direct service to these families. "I can be sitting in my office and I might hear a family checking in at the front desk, or hear kids talking and laughing. You meet people who come here under the worst of circumstances and you see the resilience of the human spirit and the kindness of strangers. It's remarkable what the families go through and every day I get to witness the power of what true community is."

But not all the moments at the Ronald McDonald House lift spirits, some challenge the very depths of your soul.

Brooke and her Mom

Consider Brooke Shockley, a 14-year-old girl who had just been diagnosed with bone cancer when she came to the House. She ended up staying there for 15 months, Sandy and her team were part of her entire journey. Brooke and her mom became part of the family. Cancer got the best of Brooke and when she died, it was as Sandy describes it, "devastating." But the spirit of the House and the care Brooke received from Sandy and her staff brought about redemption.

At the one-year anniversary of her passing, Brooke's mom, Brooke's brother and sister came back to the House and presented Sandy with Brooke's jersey from the Red Shoe Shuffle, an RMH event for which Brooke had served as honorary chairperson. But there was more. Brooke's family presented a gift to the entire staff, a Build-a-Bear which when you press the bear's hand it triggers a voice from inside the bear...it was Brooke's voice, recorded just before she died, thanking the entire staff at the Ronald McDonald House.

Brooke Lauren

Sandy and her team had served their mission; they couldn't affect Brooke's outcome, but they brought such joy to her journey, that even as she knew she was going to die, she felt compelled to say "thank you" and to leave behind her message of hope. It's moments like these which are at the very soul of the Ronald McDonald House.

And at this moment in time, under Sandy's stewardship, may be a turning point in the 30+ year history for RMH of Baltimore. The House can only host 36 families a night. Last year, 1,400 families came through the doors, but 600 more had to be turned away. It is something which is tough for the staff, to make the phone call to a family in crisis and tell them there is no room for them to come to this house of hope. But change is in the wind. A search is on in earnest to find a new location for the Ronald McDonald House of Baltimore and allow for expansion to serve more families. As soon as the property can be secured, it's full steam ahead and the construction of a new future for RMH.

Find what you love to do and make sure what you do enriches the lives of other people. Sandy is living her purpose, living her dream, living her why. "I am manager, marketer, minister, politician, business owner...I can't believe all these things exist in one job and I think about that every day," says Sandy. "Honestly, I am the luckiest person in the world to have this job."

No doubt. But hundreds, if not thousands of other people will take that same statement and turn it around, they are the lucky ones, because they have been touched by someone determined to make a difference in their lives, to bring hope, love and joy to their journey.

That someone is Sandy Pagnotti.

Until next time, thanks for taking the time.

The Sunday Series: Rich Polt & Talking GOOD

I derive joy from recognizing that which makes other people special. So when Mark asked me to be featured as the 9th installment in his upstart Sunday Series, I was touched. Sometimes the recognizer needs to feel recognized. For several years I had been dedicating my resources and free time towards creating a web platform that interviewed "change-makers" — people making a difference in the world. The work was something I was passionate about, but often I felt like the proverbial tree in the middle of the forest. Mark's amazing post came as a much needed dose of recognition and validation. It told me that what I was doing had not gone unnoticed and it helped inspire me. Thank you Mark.

–Rich Polt

It's not enough to talk the talk, you've got to walk the walk.

It's not enough to communicate, you've got to connect.

It's not enough to speak, you have to listen. It's not enough to get through, you've to get up and make a difference.

How many of us in life look at a situation and think "what's in it for me?"

It's human nature. But special people can look at the same circumstances and think, "what's in it for them?" There are heroes among us, sometimes angels and one man is here to share their story.

Meet Rich Polt.

Rich is here to show you how it's done. It's his passion, his purpose, his why. But it's all about turning the spotlight around, not to shine on him, but to shine on others who are doing great things, inspiring us all. But how do you let the world know about these "do-gooders," these purpose-driven individuals who are lighting the way? Well, you need only their story and an internet connection...and you've got Talking GOOD, (www.talkinggood.com), and the PR firm Communicate GOOD, (www.communicategood.com).

A Baltimore native, Rich has been in the business of PR for 20 years. But while most of us know PR as Public Relations, Rich has managed to bring new meaning to PR —how about Public Recognition? Rich says, "everything I do professionally and philanthropically is tied in some way to this most basic of human needs (recognition). Whether I am working to create visibility for my paying clients, or helping to drive awareness for someone on Talking GOOD, the fundamental deliverable I have to offer is recognition. I fundamentally believe that GIVING recognition to others is the most powerful way to engage individual constituents and build enduring communities."

People making a difference

Rich's newest website, Talking GOOD creates a platform that lets anyone recognize people who think they are making a difference in the world. In the words of Edith Wharton, "There are two ways of spreading light: to be the candle, or the mirror that reflects it." Rich wants Talking GOOD to be a giant mirror anyone can use when they find a candle.

There are plenty of examples of these candles burning bright: Daniel Brannon, who escaped a life of drugs and prison and now dedicates his free time to addiction counseling, (http://www.talkinggood.com/profiles/danielbrannon), or Katie Stagliano, the 14-year-old hunger activist who recently became the youngest recipient ever of the Clinton Global Citizen Award for Leadership in Civil Society, (http://www.talkinggood.com/profiles/KStagliano).

And then there's Joe Jones.

Joe was a typical "deadbeat" dad, living the life of an $800-a-day drug addict, his only goal was his next high, it certainly wasn't centered around being there for his family or for his son. But things started to change for Joe the day his son looked him in the eye and said, "I hate you." And it wasn't some spoiled teen shouting about not getting his way, it was a gut-wrenching, emotional message from a son letting his absent father know exactly what he thought of him. These are words no parent ever wants to hear, but Joe knew he deserved to hear it... and from that point on he got to work. Joe is now a national crusader for responsible fatherhood and healthy families. He is the Founder, President & CEO of Baltimore City's highly impactful Center for Urban Families (CFUF), Joe and his team "strengthen urban communities by helping fathers and families achieve stability and economic success."

(http://www.communicategood.com/2013/06/talking-good-with-joe-jones/)

Joe turned his life around and Rich Polt and Talking GOOD let us know.

These are the types of stories Rich wants to share, stories he wants you to know about, and wants you to tell him about. Rich is pursuing his life's passion, which as anyone who tries it can tell you—it's not easy, but it's worth it. "If there was some sort of scale that could measure the emotional highs and lows connected with pursuing one's own passion, it would probably look like an EKG," Rich says. "I spend so much time and energy trying to shine the spotlight on inspiring people. When you put that kind of passion out into the world and you feel like no one really cares...it can sting a bit. But then all it takes is a single positive e-mail, or a comment or a re-tweet and you realize somebody cares. And if somebody cares, then I know it's possible for a lot of people to care."

We all need to care. It's the very thread which binds our lives together. The thread can be thin, fragile, but words have power, stories bring our hearts closer, combine those two with hard work and passion and just maybe you can change the world, if you simply pay attention. Rich Polt and Talking GOOD are on a mission to do just that. Rich is taking his professional skill sets and using his writing and PR skills in the service of inspiring others, in the hopes of making a difference. Give him credit, even sharing one story is making a difference. Everything counts.

Rich, Samuel, Ethan & Jennifer Polt

We can all learn a lesson here. As Rich explains, "we are each granted a finite amount of days, some more, some less, therefore doing something– anything– is a much better option than sitting in indecision or procrastination. It's only by doing things that we learn what works and what doesn't work, what we love and what we hate. I've been on this professional journey for 20 years now and I still have no idea where it's going to take me. But I try to keep moving it forward every single day."

That's what matters. If you move forward, if you believe, if you look to enrich the lives of others, the universe will conspire on your behalf. The world will organize around your mission. Miracles can happen. GOOD is the goal. Talking GOOD. Communicate GOOD. Talk the talk, walk the walk. Listen. Communicate. Connect. Pay attention. Think of others who are passionate about making a difference in the lives of others. I can think of one man, but he wants you to think of others.

Do Rich a favor, do us all a favor, keep an eye out for those who are making it happen, those who are changing lives. People like to be inspired. Even better yet, do it yourself, then let us all know about your journey. Prove to everyone you are meant for more. Do that one thing and we all win.

Then let Rich know the story. He will share it with the world. Only GOOD can come from it all.

Until next time, thanks for taking the time.

The Sunday Series: All in for Life

"I saw Mark's Sunday Series on Facebook and was motivated to bring my stepdaughter's plight to Mark's attention, after seeing the sensitivity that he showed writing about the life challenges of others. It takes a village to provide the emotional support to uplift one's spirits and the first posting in his blog attracted a village of followers providing well wishes and comforting comments to give Debbie a needed emotional boost. Mark's engaging dialogue made a connection with her readers, these readers were strangers, thousands of them who wanted to know more about Debbie Fink Green. I wanted to make the public more aware of this rare cancer in hopes of increasing funding for research; little did I know the blog would provide a community of support for Debbie on this dreadful journey. Thank you Mark."

–Rebecca Kaplan Fink

You've heard the expression what are you willing to die for? Well, what are you *willing* to *live* for? Debbie Fink can tell you because she's going all in to try and do just that...to simply live.

Debbie's story was first brought to my attention by her stepmom Becky, who sent me an e-mail a few weeks ago:

"Your blog has motivated me to bring my stepdaughter's plight to the attention of your readers. My stepdaughter, Debbie has been struggling for almost three years with the life changes of having appendix cancer and the uncertainty of one's life expectancy. The reason I am submitting my stepdaughter's blog is to educate the public of some of the rare types of cancers that fortunately do not affect a vast number of innocent people, but unfortunately, impacts the availability of funds for any clinical trials to begin to find a

cure. As Debbie's stepmother, I equate her cancer as the step-cancer not always getting the attention it truly deserves. Debbie deals with this misfortunate roll of the dice with strength, which by the way is tattooed on the side of her foot, in that she gets up every day to live for today and not dwell on tomorrow."

Debbie Fink deserves attention, as does her fight and her strength.

It's true, her cancer is rare, only 1,000 people a year are diagnosed with appendiceal cancer. In Debbie's case, it also comes along with poorly differentiated signet ring cells. They say G-d doesn't deal you more than you can handle, so maybe a rare cancer happens only to certain people... those who have the incredible strength and fortitude greater than many could muster. Debbie is proving to be a rare individual indeed.

Her journey began just a short time after her marriage to David Green.

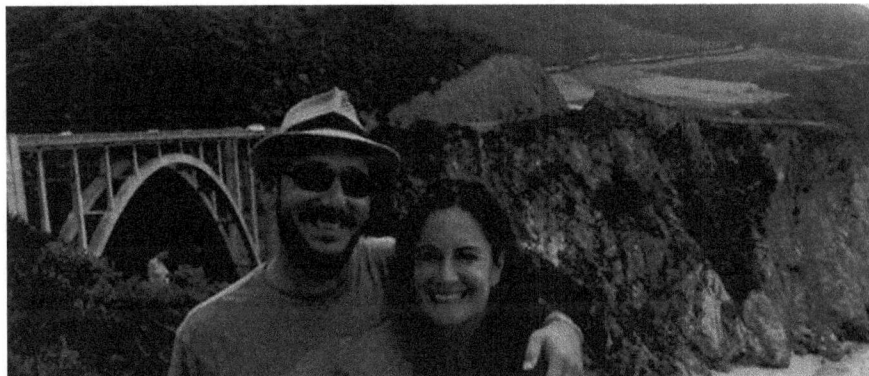

David and Debbie met at a Camp Saginaw reunion in 2008. They didn't remember each other from the camp days, but at the reunion, they connected and it wasn't too long before they were ready to make new memories they would remember, together. Debbie and David were married at the same campsite in May of 2011. But the honeymoon didn't last long. Three months after the wedding, Debbie went to the doctor to get checked for an enlarged ovary. Her goal was to get pregnant in the near future and the gynecologist assured her she could do that with just one ovary, but what was supposed to be a 45-minute laparoscopic procedure took a nasty turn, because two hours later Debbie's right ovary and her appendix were removed. Both had questionable masses on them.

Questionable soon turned to devastating.

Tests on the masses showed stage-4 appendiceal cancer. Debbie says she was "overwhelmed and sad." Treatment options were few. But Debbie decided to get aggressive. "When it's your own life, you do anything it takes to keep going." Her first surgery was January 2012, a controversial procedure called HIPEC, (Hyperthermic Intraperitoneal Chemotherapy).

"I was on the operating table for almost 10 hours," says Debbie. "Basically, once they cut me open my organs were given a heated chemotherapy bath for 90 minutes." I had a full hysterectomy and minor resections of my bladder, rectum and vagina. My surgery was deemed a success, and it was determined that I was cancer-free."

Debbie says that diagnosis did not quell her fear. "Fear ruled my life for a year after the surgery and it's not healthy, it put a strain on my marriage and my friends didn't want to be around me." Unfortunately, those fears were not unwarranted. This past summer the cancer returned and tomorrow, January 6th, Debbie will undergo a massive operation at MD Anderson Hospital in Houston, Texas which might be her only shot at survival. "I was told my best chance for the longest possible life would be a full pelvic exenteration, which would leave me with no bladder, rectum or vagina. At least, the doctor rationalized, it will buy me a few years before the cancer returns again."

Debbie says the cancer, her cancer-free days and the eventual return of the beast has made her understand you can't control everything, but you can control your reactions to everything and you really do have to count your blessings. She says her husband David has been her rock and her two stepdaughters, Zoe and Alex are taking it in stride, though not too much is spoken in their presence. Social media is also making a difference. Sometimes an internet connection can be a life-saver. Debbie says she feels like she has the support of thousands, not just her close family and friends. There is a closed Facebook group of about a thousand people who share the same cancer diagnosis and offer mental and emotional support and hope. There are stories of many in that group with 12-15 year survival rates.

Debbie has shared her journey in a few blog posts which have been picked up by Huffington Post (http://www.huffingtonpost.com/debbie-fink/) and she has a Caringbridge page where she shares updates and thoughts on the journey, (http://www.caringbridge.org/visit/debbiefinkgreen). She says post surgery she would love to get back in shape, run a 10-K, write a memoir, maybe do some more traveling. But there is no big bucket list.

"What doesn't *kill you makes you stronger,*" those are the words from the Kelly Clarkson song Debbie says she finds inspiring. The lyrics ring true. She is scared and there are still a ton of questions about post-surgery prognosis because of the rarity of the cancer, but she appreciates everyone's thoughts and prayers as she battles back from one of life's greatest challenges.

Life and survival–being there for David and the girls is the ultimate goal. The challenge Debbie is facing puts life in perspective for all of us. We all face challenges, if there isn't a road bump or obstacle in your journey through this life, you probably aren't really living. But some road blocks are bigger than others, they simply take your breath away, they try to take you down for the count. That's when you show what you are really made of. How do you rise up and fight? How do you show what you are willing to live for? Debbie Fink is facing the challenge head on, by choosing to sacrifice to save her life. The outcome is not in her hands, perhaps not really in the hands of the doctors and surgeons, though they will do all they can to get this right and to prolong Debbie's days on this earth. Maybe there could even be another miracle on the horizon...cancer-free. But like Debbie says she has learned you can't focus on what you can't control. Cancer, any type of cancer has its own agenda, its own plan and the focus needs to be on how you will react, not on the outcome.

As the author of this blog, I can control one thing as well. With surgery set for tomorrow, I would make a simple request. Keep Debbie in your thoughts and prayers. She is a warrior on the front lines and sometimes the positive thoughts of many can create the good karma Debbie deserves to see this through.

After all, Debbie is all in... for life.

Until next time, thanks for taking the time.

(Update: In life there are no guarantees. The only fact is to expect the unexpected, or to know that even in battle, no matter how hard you fight, no matter how tough your resolve and your resiliency, sometimes there on the front lines, your journey comes to an end.

About a year after this blog was written the battle got the best of Debbie Fink Green. The cancer beast claimed another victim and the world lost a good one, at least in her physical presence on this earth. But her story, her spirit, the lives she touched and her inspiration, is immortal. That's when you know you have lived a life of significance.)

The Sunday Series: Aiden's Gift

My family and I feel we are blessed that Mark picked us to write our story. Not many people have heard of Spinal Muscular Atrophy (SMA) or have seen someone affected by it. Mark helped provide us a way to let the world know about this horrible incurable disease. The amount of love and support I received after sharing our story was amazing. It made me realize I was a strong teen mother and I truly did the best for my child. I feel that with our story being told Aiden was able to touch more people's lives in 4 months and 26 days then some people can in a lifetime! Thank you for sharing our story in Aiden's memory.

—Ashley Navitskis

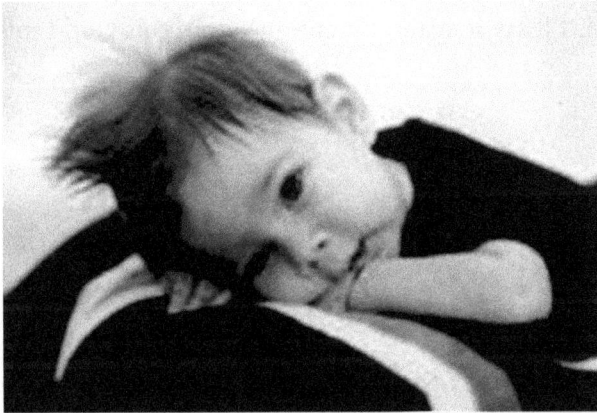

Upon first glance, this is a story I wasn't sure I wanted to tackle. But it might be the most important story you ever read.

A few months before she was to turn 18, Ashley Navitskis gave birth to Aiden James. It wasn't where Ashley thought she would be in her life, learning she was pregnant just days before her 17th birthday, it was a shocking disappointment to her parents and to Ashley. And let me be clear, teen pregnancy is not the focus of this blog, no one is taking sides, I know it's a touchy subject, but it's what happened to Aiden that might just save a life. That is where I am going to take you.

Let me just say this, and this is where the entire story turned for me– when I asked Ashley the question how she felt when she learned she was pregnant – "terrified as any young teen mom would be. I was going to be a single parent, still living at home," said Ashley. "But if you take the responsibility to have sex when you are a teenager, then accept the responsibility to be a parent." A strong statement from a young lady still shy of her 20th birthday. Aubrey Navitskis, Ashley's mom, explains her own emotions: "It was almost like we didn't have time to think too much about her being a young pregnant girl, once it happened you deal with it.

You have to move on and keep going, there's nothing you can do to change what happened. We had to get over it pretty quickly because there was a baby coming fast."

Fast forward to December 2nd, 2011...at 7 pounds, 10 ounces, Aiden James is born. I'll say it again, his entrance into this world might just save a life.

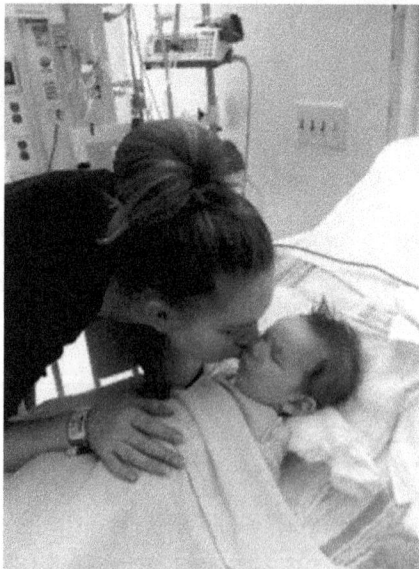

From the very beginning, there was something unusual. Ashley says Aiden was circumcised as a baby and barely let out a whimper. A short time later, when they were leaving the hospital Aiden was choking and turning blue, but the hospital staff said that could easily happen with a newborn and sent the family on their way. During his first month checkup in January, the doctor took Aiden's temperature with a rectal thermometer. Most babies scream in terror. Aiden did not move, complain or cry.

Yet for the most part Aiden acted like a typical baby, he loved to watch TV, he cried, he did almost all the things a baby likes to do, except he couldn't sleep on his back, it would create trouble with his breathing. He liked to be held a lot, and he liked to fall asleep on Ashley's chest. He always wanted Ashley.

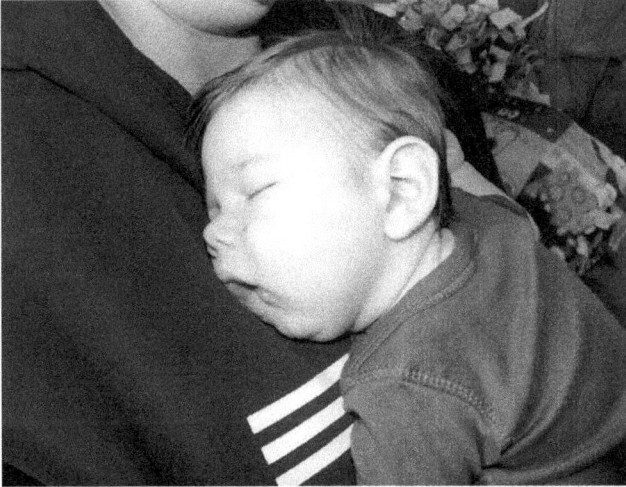

At the two-month checkup, Aiden received his first round of shots. Any parent knows it's traumatic for the infant to have needles stuck all over his/ her body. But Aiden didn't really seem to mind, his body barely became rigid, or tense as the needles were placed in his skin. But then the nurses went to give him an oral vaccine and he immediately started choking. The doctor also noticed Aiden could not hold up his head very well, or move his arms and kick his legs like a normal two-month-old. Doctor Myer said he had never seen a baby so happy and full of awareness, but unable to move the way he should. He decided it was time for a second opinion. An appointment was made with a neurologist.

It didn't take the neurology team very long. They had seen Dr. Myer's reports and after a difficult procedure to get an IV into Aiden and to extract blood for genetic testing they had a serious suspicion. But there was still one test to be completed, an EMG muscle test. But at two months old and with some muscle issues, the doctors said they could not put Aiden to sleep for the procedure, which would involve a series of shocks to his body. So they had to resort to giving him pain medications every 15-to-20 minutes, then shock his body, look for a response, and then repeat. Aiden was not responding, there was no reflex, except for his crying during a torturous 45-minute procedure.

As is so often with modern medicine, the testing told the story. And concern turned a corner to catastrophic. Aiden had a motor neuron disease, the number one killer of babies before their six-month birthday... SMA – Spinal Muscular Atrophy. In Aiden's case, it was Type I, also known as Werdnig-Hoffmann Disease. A child with SMA Type I is unable to sit or stand without help. Swallowing and feeding become difficult and the child eventually loses the ability to swallow safely without aspirating, (choking or inhaling secretions and food particles into the lungs). But maybe the biggest problem is the weakness of the muscles used for breathing, those that help expand the chest and fill the lungs with air. It becomes difficult to breathe at all. Aiden was in trouble, the doctors said his testing showed this was fatal, he wouldn't live to see his 1st birthday. They gave the Navitskis family a choice, try to prolong his life with a tracheostomy and feeding tube, or choose comfort care, meaning take Aiden home with pain medication and hospice. Ashley turned to her parents for help with a decision that had to be made that day. It was decided they would take Aiden home, keep him comfortable and wait for the inevitable.

I'm proud of my Mommy!

Back at home, a group of counselors and therapists would visit a few times a week and Aiden actually seemed to be doing pretty well. As the calendar turned to April the family was actually talking about planning a trip to the beach for Mother's Day. But by late April things were changing. Aiden had episodes where he would stop breathing and turn blue. He needed oxygen and suction of his mouth almost every day, yet somehow Aiden would rebound from the procedure.

But on the night of April 25th Ashley says the family dog, Angel, did something strange. "She suddenly jumped up on the bed," says Ashley, "Angel always slept in my parents' room, but this night she wouldn't leave my room. Angel walked over to Aiden, gave him a sniff and a lick and then went and lay down at the end of the bed and refused to leave."

Morning came and Ashley's father Adam and her sister Alyssa were off for a field trip to DC. Ashley decided to give Aiden a dose of morphine, since the prior three-day period had been pretty rough. Then she lay down with Aiden like she always did and the two watched his favorite show, Tom & Jerry Kids. The hospice team was to visit later in the morning. But suddenly there was another episode, Aiden was turning blue, Ashley was bouncing him up and down on her leg, which is what she would always do when Aiden started choking. But this time it wasn't working. Ashley's mom tried to suction not just Aiden's mouth this time, but the back of his throat, it seemed to help, so Ashley and Aubrey put the oxygen mask on Aiden's face. Aiden hated that mask, but there was no choice. Aubrey said whatever crying Aiden could manage sounded like a death rattle. The end was near.

Aubrey called her husband and told him to somehow find a way to get home from the field trip because as she painfully told him on the phone, "Aiden was dying." She put the phone to Aiden's ear so Adam and Alyssa, miles away in DC, could speak to him. Aiden, with an oxygen mask on his face and still on Ashley's lap, was listening, he looked up at Ashley, looked over to Aubrey and closed his eyes. It didn't feel like he was breathing, but Ashley said she couldn't remove the mask, for fear he might still be alive, there might still be some hope. But on this day, hope had run its course.

On April 26th, 2012, Aiden died in Ashley's arms.

For any parent, it is their worst fear and greatest pain. Devastating beyond belief. Ashley can barely speak about the entire experience, but her mom Aubrey says the pain was nearly indescribable, "how do you watch your child bury their child? And a grandparents' love for that child.. I can't even describe it. Knowing you can't save your grandchild is heart wrenching, our hearts are broken, Aiden took a piece of each of our hearts. He was an amazing child."

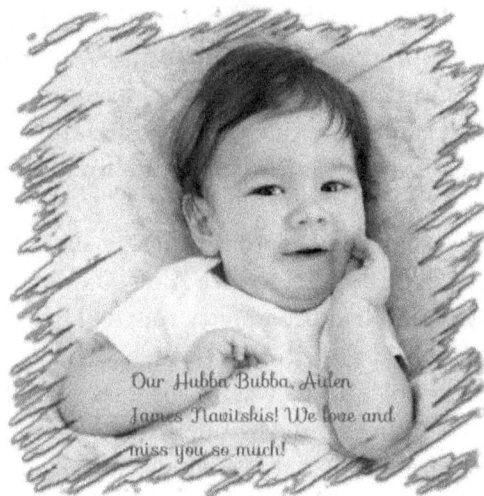

Our Hubba Bubba, Aiden James Nawitskis! We love and miss you so much!

But Aiden's mom made him a promise. Knowing he would pass on one day, Ashely told Aiden she would get her life back together. She had to drop out of high school when she learned she was pregnant and the family actually moved out of state. She promised Aiden she would go back to high school, or get her GED. Ashley did just that, she got a job, earned her GED credits, got her driver's license and now has a full-time job at a local hospital. Approaching her 20th birthday, Ashley has already lived through life's greatest tragedy. She is determined to rise back up and to make sure Aiden's life makes a difference and share her lesson: "Everyone who has a child, love them, cherish them and never take them for granted, because not every day is promised," says Ashley.

It's a tough story to tell, a tough one to read, but I said it could save a life. Understand that 1 in every 40 people carry the gene which causes SMA. If both parents are carriers there is a 1-in-4 chance the baby will suffer the same fate as Aiden, and be diagnosed with SMA-Type I. There is a simple blood test which can detect the gene. If you are thinking about having a child, you should think about finding out if you are a carrier. Ashley and Aubrey believe Aiden was here to save the life of another child and if even one other life is saved, then Aiden's story gains even greater significance.

Not that it doesn't already. Although his body had trouble moving muscle, Aiden's heart moved mountains and continues to do so even today. Sharing his story might change the life of another. It's Aiden's gift to the world.

Please go to www.fsma.org to learn more. You can also visit Ashley's facebook page @ https://www.facebook.com/ashley.navitskis?fref=ts

Until next time, thanks for taking the time.

The Sunday Series: Never Be Alone

I suddenly lost my husband of 20 years (will have been four years now on 6/14/17) - leaving behind our three beautiful children and myself! Mark was kind enough to approach me with wanting to do a story about our lives together and I graciously said, "sure!" He portrayed our family, our love, our story so beautifully - with such elegance, respect and love for us and there were times that I would just read it and it would make me cry, but also empower me. I needed a reminder here and there of my mission to get through the darkness and reading the beautiful story that Mark composed/ captured with MY words and from my heart, gave me that kick/jolt to keep moving forward! I actually just read it again before writing this - what a talented and beautiful writer Mark truly is! I almost felt the words leap from my iPad into my soul! Thank you so much for giving our children and myself a beautiful reminder of our lives together!

–Penny Kinkade

On June 14th, 2013, breathing became difficult. Oxygen was in short supply, as was any sense of rational thought, or glimmer of hope for the future, any future. Grant Kinkade was gone.

Grant and his friend Bob Rust were hit and killed the night of June 14th as they were crossing the road in Fenwick, Delaware. Just weeks before the Kinkade family had purchased their first beach house in Fenwick. Grant was a Senior Partner for New York Life in the Baltimore General Office, Bob was the father-in-law of another Partner in that same office. Today, we are not recounting all the details of what happened, you can read the back story in this post,

(http://markbrodinsky.com/2013/06/17/
when-tomorrow-never-comes-its-just-about-life/).

No, today it's about coming out of the dark.

I never met Bob, but I worked with Grant and met his wife, Penny. And that's where we travel today, on Penny's road to recovery. Courage, hope, inspiration. As Grant would tell her all the time, "baby steps and small wins."

It just so happens right before our interview, Penny had gone to do what she had put off for quite some time...picking up the urn where Grant's ashes will be placed, at least for now. Penny had not wanted to go, she had put off so many things following the loss of the man who called her "pooky" and his "princess." But Penny says for 2014 this was one of the things she needed to accomplish, handling things one day at a time. But as soon as she had her husband's ashes in her hands, the past seven months came flooding back, the reality of her life, for which sometimes she says she is still in denial... was more than she could take. She got back in the car, heard the song, "Best Friends," which meant so much to her and Grant, At that point Penny says she "lost it." But then, just like she has done over and over and over these past seven months, she collected herself, got it together and was ready to speak to me.

Courage.

Penny and Grant met more than two decades ago, while he was still working at the Giant grocery store. Penny says he "jumped into a bottle of Polo," the first time they were together, as to mask the scent he picked up at the store. Though I only spoke to Penny on the phone for this interview, I could hear her smile as she recounted those early days. "He didn't always smell the best," she said, "he smelled from the job, but the Polo made it better." Years later, when Penny would ask Grant why he smelled so good he would tell her it wasn't the Polo, it was the "Dove soap."

A certain scent, a familiar smell can invoke a special memory, yet now that's all Penny has left. The couple was 32 days shy of their 20th wedding anniversary when Grant was taken from this world. Penny compares her own life with Grant to the classic Hollywood couple, George Burns and Gracie. The legendary comedian George Burns was the down-to-earth realist, Gracie his wife, the sometimes scatter-brained dreamer. That's how many marriages work best, the hot-and-the-cold, the ying-and-the-yang, the black-and-the-white. Penny says she and Grant could trade jabs with the greatest of ease, but always had so much respect for one another, especially when it came to allowing each other to do what they enjoyed.

Penny loved to dance. Grant could care less. She says Grant would always say he was "taking one for the team," when he took her dancing. Grant had a classic line for everything. Penny would dance, he would watch and then rescue her when her other dance partners got a little too close for comfort. Or Penny said he simply had to just go get her so they could leave, because she couldn't stop dancing, or talking. "Let's go, we gotta go, we're getting old here," he would say.

In turn, Grant loved to hang out with the boys, many of those "boys" were the members of his team, the group of agents he led at New York life. The rule was if Grant called Penny, it meant it was her time to go pick him up. No drinking and driving. They would always keep each other safe. It's one of the things the Kinkade children wonder about now. Her son Tucker recently told Penny, "you did everything you could to make sure you and Dad didn't get hurt, how come that family, (the one driving the car that killed Grant), didn't?"

It's a question many are asking. But the question of "why" will forever be one that is not easy to answer and troubles Tucker and Penny's other children, Madison and Shelby. Penny says sometimes it's a perfect storm of grief. Yet it's Penny, who has tried at times to mask the grief from her children. She's the one hiding in the closet to cry until she is called to help with a family activity, or to answer a question, then wipe the tears and appear to be calm and collected. Friends are telling her it's ok to show the sadness, after all the kids need to see just how much their parents loved each other.

Talking to Penny, there is little doubt about devotion and endless love. Grant was a big man, but despite his gruff exterior and imposing presence, he had the softest of hearts for his wife, son and daughters. He never forgot his most important responsibilities were husband, father, coach, provider. He was meticulous, a planner and a success story, having gone from the grocery store to become an insurance agent, then moving up the ranks to Senior Partner. His "minions" as Penny called them, loved him as much as his own family did. Current and former agents are telling her stories of how Grant changed their lives and continues to do so, even after his passing. What others may have taken for granted, they are now embracing simply because of what happened to the Kinkade family.

Penny says so many people tell her how they now go home earlier to spend time with their family, they don't work so hard, they live in the moment, they make sure they are family-focused because they realize how lives can be changed in an instant. "I'm happy for them," says Penny, "but so sad we had to experience this loss for others to find out what is important. I always believed everything happens for a reason, but I'm not really getting it right now. I'm really having a hard time understanding why this happened. Not just Grant, but Bob too. Bob beat cancer and everybody loved him. Two amazing people gone in one fell swoop. Wow. They made such an impact here on earth, maybe God wanted them to be with Him."

At times that faith and belief carry Penny through the day. Other times it's therapy, books and friends who are helping Penny to cope. You don't spend 23 years with someone, lose him and then a little more than half-a-year later suddenly see the world as rosy, but Penny has already overcome a significant challenge. She is coming out of the dark, her own rage. It's a lesson she says she wants to share.

"It almost happened to me," says Penny. "I almost let anger consume me. I started hating everything. I hated that the trees were green, the grass was green, everything and anything I saw and it scared me. I always told Grant I am a survivor. I am not the little engine that could, I am the little engine that can." And so Penny is making it happen, for herself, for her children and for life. "It sucks he is not here and I hate he is not here. But I have such a zest for life. Grant always told me baby steps and small wins, baby steps and small wins. All you need is a win and you will rock whatever you decide to do."

So Penny is making her decision to tackle the challenges before her head on. As the calendar turns to 2014, she is committed to tackling one thing at a time, day by day. On the day we spoke it was the challenge of picking up the urn, "a win," she says. It's one more thing she can check off her list of challenges, emotional, mental and even physical, to keep her life and the lives of Madison, Shelby and Tucker moving forward. Penny says she and Grant were not a "normal couple" because they had been together so long. Then again, "normal" is relative for any relationship. It's all about love, conviction, dedication and compromise. Penny says Grant kept her on track. "I was always running late and he hated that, but he dealt with it because it was me. I would get lost a lot, I could get lost in my own backyard. Grant was my compass, my moral compass, he was my everything. I'm starting over again. I'm on the see-saw, but it's not moving, because I don't have a counterpart. Who is going to get me like he did? He just got me, he just did."

What Penny may not realize, but I could tell in the time we spoke, is just how far she has come. She is able to perfectly articulate her situation, talk about the accident, talk about the challenges she and her children face and I could hear the sadness and sense of loss in her voice, but also that of determination. Like Penny says, she has a "zest for life" and she reminds herself of that and all that she needs to accomplish. She also realizes she is doing the one thing Grant would want her to do, to carry on, she has something to prove to him. "I'm doing this for him," says Penny. "He is happy now, he was sad because he had to leave us, but I know he is happy now. And I'm doing this for him. I want him to see I can do this. I want him to know I was always listening. I was paying attention. Baby steps and small wins."

Sometimes the synergy with this blog and the Sunday Series is off the charts. When Penny spoke of Grant as being her compass, I was quickly reminded of a video I saw just a few days before from the group Lady Antebellum. The name of that song? *Compass*. Those lyrics are as if Grant were speaking to Penny. I'm including some of them here, but I challenge you to click on the YouTube link below, then get ready to stand up, clap your hands, dance, and celebrate, because that's what Grant would have wanted.

I knew Grant well enough to know he would not want any pity parties... just a reason to party and then get out there and make life happen. Just like Penny is doing for him now. "I'm an extension of Grant," she says. Which means his heart will go on.

Baby steps and small wins.

You want to give up cause it's dark, we're really not that far apart. So let your heart, sweetheart, be your compass when you're lost, you should follow it wherever it may go. When it's all said and done, you can walk instead of run, cause no matter what you'll never be alone.

Never be alone – Compass, lyrics by Lady Antebellum

(https://www.youtube.com/watch?v=oiG-4-V7Xd0)

Until next time, thanks for taking the time.

The Sunday Series: Hold Onto My Heart

When I was introduced to Mark by my nephew I was not sure if I could or even wanted to share my story. Being grief stricken, very fragile and emotionally exhausted from the entire experience of a huge loss, I just wasn't sure. Jason, my nephew, thought it would be good for me. So I did.

Speaking to Mark was easy. Mark Brodinsky was able to put my story into words that just were perfect. When the story was posted on the Sunday Series I read and re-read. It was viewed by family and friends that just loved it. It has helped me in so many ways. I go back to it often, when I do, it now feels warm and inviting. That's what Mark's story has done for me. I will be ever grateful for meeting such a wonderful person that I consider my friend.

–Gail Parker

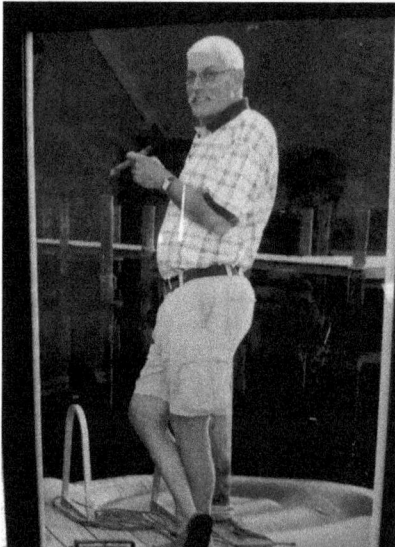

It happens every day, though we frequently don't notice, or are simply not aware. A light is kindled, another extinguished. One soul enters this world, another exits.

Light, life and Craig Wehrle, a perfect match. Craig grabbed onto life with both hands and gave it everything he had. Navy man, businessman, mason, sailor, hunter, father, grandfather, uncle, friend, soul mate. Gail Parker knows all about what made Craig "dynamic, powerful and alive," she spent two decades by his side. The two brought their respective families together in perfect harmony. Though Craig and Gail never married, it wasn't because they didn't want to.

Life just got in the way.

A visit to the podiatrist because of a blister on Craig's toe led to a referral to a vascular doctor and eventually a neurologist. Tests run, results deciphered, the doctor said Craig had peripheral neuropathy, a condition which can distort and sometimes interrupt messages between the brain and the rest of the body. The doctor put Craig on steroids. It was a Band-Aid for what was ailing him, but the journey inside the journey of Craig's life was now underway.

A tough man, a war veteran, Craig Wehrle served in the Navy in Vietnam. At one point, spending four solid months in a submarine. His experience taught him to love the water and when he left the Navy, he was ready to sail again. Craig bought a 32-foot Morgan (built by the legendary Charles Morgan), called Lulu, named after the cartoon character Little Lulu. For Craig and for Gail the open waters were magic. They both loved to sail and spent a tremendous amount of time with Lulu, riding her and working on her.

But as the illness took a turn and the "drop-foot" started for Craig, the sailing started to subside. From experiencing trouble with his foot, to walking with a cane and then to a walker, Craig's mobility was waning. Eventually, Gail bought Craig a scooter chair so he could get around quickly, it was important, it was necessary, because besides his love of the water, Craig also loved something else...to work, to provide.

A mechanical engineer by trade, Craig ran his own business then sold it and went into property management, eventually managing a 33-story high-rise, the Penthouse Condominium in Towson, Maryland. The position was not for the weak of heart, nor for someone without stamina, because dealing with more than 300 affluent condo owners, Craig rarely sat still. It wasn't part of his DNA anyway, he loved not only to sail, but to hunt and to be part of the Masons fraternity. Craig was the Grand Master of his lodge, Liberty 219 Grand Lodge of Mason. For those who might not know, the main principles of Freemasonry insist that each member show tolerance, respect and kindness in his actions toward others; practices charity and care for the community as a whole; and strives to achieve high moral standards in his own personal life. The Masons, their mission, the opportunity to care and give back fit Craig to a tee.

What didn't fit with Gail was what was happening to Craig. A man so mobile, so agile, so strong, now had trouble even climbing the stairs. The doctors Craig was working with to battle their diagnosis of neuropathy said they were having success using chemotherapy as a treatment. Gail and Craig were planning to take a trip, they had purchased the airline tickets, ready to go to overseas to Italy, and to get married. But the couple, searching for a ray of light, hoping to improve Craig's lot in life, canceled the trip and decided to give chemo a try. The first round of chemotherapy, every Friday for ten weeks, brought what the couple believed to be a glimmer of hope, some feeling, some tingling in Craig's left leg. But not much more.

The second round of chemo beat him down. Gail says Craig couldn't do much more than sleep and still find a way to get to work. Gail says watching Craig simply get to his car in the morning was tough enough:

"A man who was so agile, a sailor, if you saw the things he did on the sailboat, handle the lines, climb up and down the mast and now he was having a hard time just walking to his car. It broke my heart." Gail decided what the doctors were doing wasn't working and she was going to take action. Talking with Gail Parker, you can tell she's a woman of action.

Gail searched and got in contact with Dr. Vinay Chaudhry of Johns Hopkins. She secured an appointment four months down the road. Gail wanted more information, more help, willing to do whatever it took to find a way to help Craig get better. But time was not on their side. Is it really for any of us? The one thing in life which is completely out of our control, though we search in vain for ways to make time stand still, especially when someone we love is failing...to stop the precious moments from ticking away. Craig was getting worse and by July of 2012, the powers that be told Craig his work in property management was over.

September 17th of that same year, Gail and Craig and their respective families met Dr. Chaudhry. After a nerve connectivity test, the doctor asked them a question, one which would bring hope to an end. Dr. Chaudhry, a Professor of Neurology, had a few areas of expertise, one of those was dealing with Amyotrophic Lateral Sclerosis. "Did anyone talk to you about ALS?" Dr. Chaudhry asked the family. Gail said the other doctors told her multiple times Craig's condition was not ALS, it was peripheral neuropathy, which is why they had been searching for treatment to improve his life. Dr. Chaudhry said not only was this ALS, it was aggressive. Hope– which Craig, Gail and their respective families held onto was no longer the word of the day. The focus now was hospice, hospice at home.

Gail says Craig told her, "I don't want to leave you, but I don't want to live like this and put you through this. I can't walk for myself, I can't care for myself and I don't want to put you and the family through this."

On December 22nd, just three months after the official diagnosis of ALS, Craig was gone.

Gail still harbors anger, saying she has little faith in the medical system. She believes Craig was put through the mill with misdiagnosis and mishandled - because of this the family had little time to prepare for the inevitable. But Gail is also giving back for good. She says the MDA, The Muscular Dystrophy Association, reached out during Craig's ordeal and Gail has formed Team Craig for the annual walk. Last year she raised $6,000, second most of any team which participated and this year she is striving to be the number one fundraising team for the MDA. The goal, to find a cure for one of the most debilitating of diseases.

http://mda.org/?gclid=CIr26o-l4rwCFcY7OgodfwEA3A

Gail and Craig's son Jason have also gotten his beloved boat Lulu back in the water, renamed her Lulu Ann, for Gail's middle name and the middle name of Craig's granddaughter Morgan. They plan to spread Craig's ashes along some of the places Craig and Gail visited together along the Chesapeake.

Gail now sails through life without her partner saying she is, "haunted by the experience. But the goodness that comes out of something like this is the family and strength of the family I still have by my side, we've continued a very strong bond and that's wonderful." Part of that family and extended family are Gail's nephew Jason and his wife, Xian. On December 22nd, Jason and Xian, about to have their first child, came to visit Craig in the hospital. Craig had been overjoyed for his nephew and niece and their impending bundle of joy. On the day he died, Craig was heavily medicated, nearly in a coma, the sight upset Xian, and upon returning home, her water broke. She gave birth to Hailey that same day.

Gail says she learned of the news and received pictures on her phone. Gail climbed into the hospital bed with Craig, spoke to him, let him know Jason and Xien had a baby girl, named Hailey. She asked Craig to open his eyes to see, Gail says she thought he did, saw them flutter, but she knows he heard her and the announcement. At 7:11, exactly two hours after learning of the news of Hailey's birth, Craig took his final breath.

A light kindled, a light extinguished. A soul entering this world, a soul exiting. Such is life, it happens more often than we know.

Until next time, thanks for taking the time.

The Sunday Series: Believe in Tomorrow

Mark Brodinsky's sharing of the Believe In Tomorrow Children's Foundation story has helped to bring much needed attention to the many challenges faced by children with cancer and their families. Like a beacon of light in the shadowy world of the unknown, Mark's ability to share our story has helped families find the support they need, and has brought much needed hope to their lives.

—Brian Morrison

"I worked for the University of Maryland and I was assigned to the Shock Trauma center for a three month period of time. The pediatric oncology clinic was on the same floor and as you left Shock Trauma, you would see the oncology clinic. I had never really seen sick kids before, I was in my mid 20's and wanted to do something a little more positive with my life, so I started volunteering and became very interested in the gaps which existed in providing services to families."

Those are the words of Brian Morrison, who more than 30 years ago had a wish. He put time into that wish, turned it into a dream and made that dream a reality, a reality called Believe in Tomorrow. (http://www.believeintomorrow.org/)

For more than half his life, Brian has championed the cause. He formed the Believe in Tomorrow Foundation and set up a hospital housing facility for critically ill children and their families...children who are receiving treatment at Johns Hopkins Hospital in Baltimore. But that is just scratching the surface of what makes the foundation unique.

What truly sets the Believe in Tomorrow Foundation apart, is the opportunity it offers to give families a break. A break from what at times seems like a never-ending cycle of treatment, worry and fatigue. It began with a single condo on the beaches of Ocean City, Maryland. "In 1986 we started renting condos at the beach," says Brian "and made them available to critically ill children and their families we were seeing at the University of Maryland Hospital and Johns Hopkins. In 1986 we only had one condo, in 1987 we had three and there were six by 1988." But Brian and his team wanted to do more if they could make an entire facility like that available to families, they could fill a huge void. The centerpiece of Believe in Tomorrow was born.

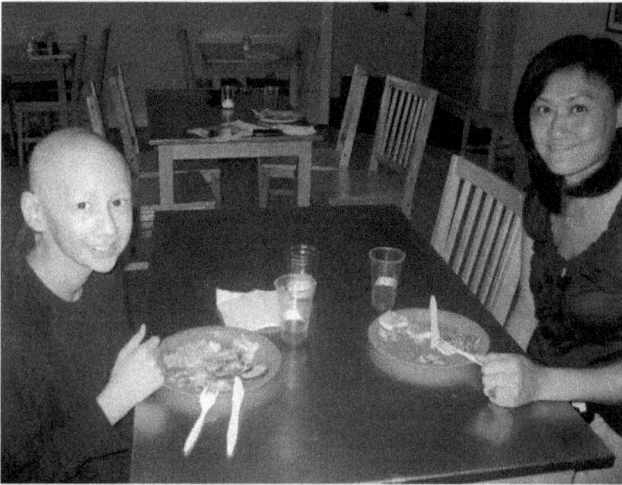

The whole point of the respite facilities is for the families and their critically ill children to experience a time away from the rigors of daily treatments and the incredible stress of that daily existence. Brian says, "we believe by doing so, by creating normalcy during a very abnormal experience, it does have a powerful impact on the healing process."

Right now there are three such facilities in Ocean City, with one planned for Bethany Beach, Delaware and another down in Florida. There is even a respite house up in the mountains at Deep Creek Lake and another down south in Asheville, North Carolina. Since 1986, thousands of critically ill children and their families have used the respite homes free of charge, to renew their energy and their spirit.

Brian says the goal of these award-winning facilities is simple, but sometimes that which seems simple is the most challenging to accomplish. The team from Believe in Tomorrow wants the families to walk into these places and say "Wow." At the beach, the condos are beautifully decorated so that everyone who arrives can enjoy and get a great night's sleep. Brian says, "it's very common for families to arrive and experience extraordinary things." The respite facilities tend to amplify the good feelings you have when you go on vacation. About 90% of the children who come to the respite homes are oncology patients who are facing an uphill battle and want nothing more than a chance to be distracted by beautiful surroundings. "We really are striving every day", says Brian, "to make a positive difference in the lives of both critically ill children and their families by creating this high level of service for them and this level of service gives them hope and comfort and the opportunity to believe in tomorrow."

The families appreciate the time away: "The long weekend was so relaxing and peaceful. Knowing that we could get away from the stress of having a child with cancer, and just be a family enjoying our time together was something we will remember for a long time." – The Family of Taylor, age 3, battling leukemia.

Like most non-profits, the goal is to raise funds and get donations to keep the program going. Brian says the Believe in Tomorrow Foundation looks to develop partnerships with corporations, individuals and others, not just for dollars, but also contributed services and materials. In 1993, the Believe in Tomorrow House at Johns Hopkins Hospital was built by 360 companies and 3,000 skilled workers who volunteered their time and materials...everything from steel, bricks, and mortar to get the building finished and ready for the families and their children who so desperately need the services.

In 2006, Believe In Tomorrow opened the door on a highly unique hospital housing facility. The Believe In Tomorrow House at St. Casimir serves as the first stand-alone hospital housing facility in the country which caters exclusively to pediatric bone marrow transplant patients. It is the first and only facility of its kind. And the giving continues.

For Brian Morrison, this is a labor of love. He says he gets a tremendous amount of enjoyment out of doing things which make a difference. And he loves the difference a group can make when they combine their efforts and work toward a common goal. "I absolutely love the spirit of people who show up to volunteer. When you can find where their talents lie and how they can help, magical things can happen."

That is the ultimate goal, to make magic. Though tomorrow is never promised, for those who need it most, the Foundation gives them a reason to believe.

Until next time, thanks for taking the time.

The Sunday Series: Hope Matters

In that one weekend Diane realized what had been missing these past years, as she has struggled to survive and most importantly to bring some sense of normalcy to life for her boys, who are growing up without a father.

–Mark Brodinsky

There is single parenting, then there is something else. Those who are forced to go it alone, by no fault of their own.

Sole parent. Not single, sole. Widow. Survivor. Different names, one distinction, doing it all...alone. The responsibility of life, not just yours, but those you helped bring into this world now relying on you, just you, to see them through.

Diane Hyatt knows what it's all about. She knows what it takes, but it wasn't until just recently, she took the time to take care of herself.

Marty Hyatt, husband, father to the couple's two young boys, passed away suddenly in May of 2009. A life lost and in the blink of an eye, three lives which needed to be rebuilt, three lives floating sometimes aimlessly in a sea of shock and heartache that only sudden death can bring. Diane says the first year was like living in a fog, trying to see through the thick mist and forge a path for her young boys, Kevin and Sean. Her sole focus; to be a sole parent and give the boys the life they deserve.

MEMORIES OF YOU WILL NEVER FADE AWAY,
BUT GET STRONGER EVERY DAY

MARTY HYATT
5/24/65 - 5/7/09

Parenting with two partners can be tough enough. Going it alone, Diane says the challenges are many: "I am always questioning myself. Am I raising the kids the way Marty would have wanted me to raise them? Am I doing the right thing? I'm having the tough discussions, the financial concerns. I constantly worry and want to know I am guiding them in the right direction, hoping I am giving them the tools to live a great life, making sure I am doing the right thing." The worry, the concern, the focus on her boys, now ages 17 and 13, never ends. And that focus for the past five years, the life of a young widow, has taken its toll.

Diane says she has tremendous support from family and friends, but the questions are always the same, "how are the boys, how are you?" It's really no one's fault, most times others don't know what to say. They feel legitimate concern, but Diane says it's tough to answer the same inquiries over and over. She says since most people aren't living the life of a young widow, they just "don't get it." And she has been so busy raising her two boys on her own, she didn't get it either. The "it" being time for her to grieve and to grow. Then she found Camp Widow.

(http://www.campwidow.org/)

You are not alone.

SSLF.org
Connecting widowed people

"It took me five years," says Diane, "to do something for myself." She says she learned about the program about a year ago. Camp Widow is just one of the events held by the organization, Soaring Spirits International, (http://www.sslf.org/). The focus of the organization... hope matters. It's goal; to help widows realize they are not alone, a feeling Diane and many like her have to overcome. Each year nearly 800,000 people around the world are forced to go it alone. Soaring Spirits seeks to connect widowed people with each other. It's all about community. It's the relief of being understood by another widowed person, getting the opportunity to laugh, to cry, to have access to hope and help transform the person whose life has been forever altered by death.

Diane returned from her first Camp Widow experience just last week and her biggest takeaway she says, "they get it, they just get it." For the first time in five years, Diane was no longer being asked the same questions by those who mean well, but don't live the day-to-day struggle of sole parenting, of knowing what it's like to be a young widow. The founder of Soaring Spirits, Michele Hernandez, a woman just like Diane, shares the same struggle.

At only 37, Michele lost her husband and was left with two young children. She started Soaring Spirits because she found few to talk with who suffered the loss of a spouse. Camp Widow is part of the healing process, a light to find a way out of the fog, to resurface from the depths of despair, buoyed by others who are there to hold you up because they are living the same. For Diane, Camp Widow did just that, including a moment she will long remember, because it is one she had put off for so long.

On the final night of the three-day event, the 150 widows in attendance were given an assignment, write a message to the one you loved and lost. These survivors took the time to share their true feelings, then folded them up into origami boats and released them into the waters near their hotel. Diane says it was incredible to see all those paper boats and messages heading out into the harbor in a flotilla of love and of hope. The moment was overwhelming. On that paper boat was a message from Diane and her boys to Marty. She told him so many things she had wanted to say over the past five years, but had never taken the time to do so. "It was huge for me," says Diane. "I didn't realize how emotional it was to be able to do that."

In that one weekend, Diane realized what had been missing these past years, as she has struggled to survive and most importantly to bring some sense of normalcy to life for her boys, who are growing up without a father. Diane says before she made the definite decision to travel to Camp Widow, she first talked to Kevin and Sean. And the first thing both boys told their mother, "Mom you need to go, you need to go, you never do anything for yourself." Diane says the weekend she was away the boys were solely responsible for themselves, but it was her they worried about. She says the boys called or sent texts to her constantly to make sure she was OK. Diane says her sons are so protective of her because they have already suffered a tremendous loss, their greatest fear is to lose another.

The love and concern Kevin and Sean feel for their mom is a testament to the sacrifices she has made to make their world whole, despite the emptiness and loneliness she has struggled to overcome. But Diane says the weekend at Camp Widow turned her sense of loss into one of hope.

"Knowing there are other people out there who have suffered the same and feel the same is so important to me. They love to hug at Camp Widow, they get it, they just get it."

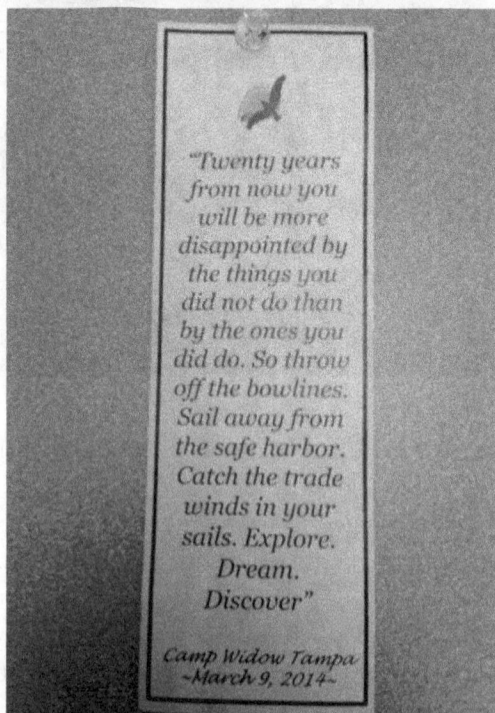

"Twenty years from now you will be more disappointed by the things you did not do than by the ones you did do. So throw off the bowlines. Sail away from the safe harbor. Catch the trade winds in your sails. Explore. Dream. Discover"

Camp Widow Tampa
~March 9, 2014~

To know you are not alone is a powerful feeling for anyone going through this journey we call life. But experience a great loss and that feeling of community can be a life-saver. For Diane, for other widows just like her, sole parents thrust into a world of making it OK for others, there is a great lesson. As Diane learned it's alright to make it OK for yourself, to reconnect with who you are and get back on track. Diane says she hopes her experience and her story can inspire others to "do something for yourself, find hope, learn to love yourself so you can move on."

As Diane has learned in a world where challenges abound– big and small – hope matters.

Until next time, thanks for taking the time.

The Sunday Series: In Full Bloom, Again

Poppy, here I am. It's my big day. The night I wrote this, I came downstairs crying to my Mom about how I didn't remember you enough. I remember you cooking us eggs, lox and onions in the morning. I remember the feeling of your prickly beard. I remember you sitting by the ocean while we collected seashells. But I think the only thing I need to remember is how much you loved us, and still do.

–Sophie Brodinsky

The focus of this series, real stories, your stories is to provide perspective on life, through others who are showing us the way with their courage, hope and inspiration. My daughters do this every day by their very existence, because they have given me life's most precious gift, the ability to experience unconditional love from the moment they arrived. Every kiss good morning, every hug good night, is the most simple reinforcement of a love which is truly beyond words.

They also teach me. And one year ago today, my oldest, Sophie, taught me one of my most important lessons, one so strong, it provided me not only the final inspiration but also the signature line for my book: "speak from the heart and everyone who has one will buy in."

On Saturday, March 23rd, 2013, Sophie demonstrated to more than 200 people in attendance, the meaning of that sentence. Men, women, children...most sitting there listening with tears in their eyes listening to my daughter, who that day, the day of her Bat Mitzvah, truly did step into another stage of life by showing maturity and deep emotion many will long remember and I won't ever forget. That evening, in a speech she had crafted just days before, and I had never heard, she gratefully thanked nearly all of her close family and friends, those she believed in her heart, helped her get to this point in her life. It was so powerful and moving for her that when she got to the part about her grandfather, the deepest sense of loss in her young life, she needed the assistance of her tutor to move through it.

I am using this day, this Sunday, one year later to recap with a few links. At the time this blog, launched just a few months prior, was still in its infancy, and I took the opportunity to write down my own feelings about what was happening in our lives and what had turned into a trilogy of blogs that long weekend. It didn't start out that way, but progressed into such in my mind and my heart, so I went with it. The first I titled, "The (Our) Rose," the second, "In Full Bloom," the third, "Don't Stop Believing."

Below I am providing the links to the first and the third blogs. I respect your time and your own existence, so if you choose to click on those and read them, wonderful, if not, that's fine too. I believe they provide perspective on the story of that weekend, however, the second blog, "In Full Bloom," stands on its own because it was the centerpiece of the experience. The event which touched so many lives and stands today, for me, as one of the most inspirational moments of these past twelve months.

The first blog, The (Our) Rose: (http://markbrodinsky.com/2013/03/23/the-our-rose-its-just-about-life/) The third blog, Don't Stop Believing: (http://markbrodinsky.com/2013/03/26/dont-stop-believing-ts-just-about-life/)

And, the second: In Full Bloom, which I am re-posting below...

There was barely a dry eye in the room when Sophie Rose finished her thank you speech on Saturday night. She had touched people's hearts in a way that will long be remembered. There were hearts overflowing with joy and love, as she put an exclamation point on one of the most special events of our lives, and certainly of hers.

Sophie nailed it, without really even trying, because she owned it. Our daughter's Bat Mitzvah ceremony was just that, her Bat Mitzvah ceremony. After her Torah portion and an explanation of what it all meant, she shared feelings that lay deep in her heart, about those who helped her make it this far in her life. At the ripe old age of 13, my girl connected to this moment in time like I have seen few do. Granted, I am her father, but from the testimonials I have received all day from other people who were sitting in the same room as I, Sophie connected with them too. She was simply remarkable. I watched her conduct herself with poise, grace and then in an instant, tears of appreciation, gratitude and love for those closest to her and for those who had been so close, but are no longer in this world, living only in her memory and in her heart.

She broke down, but then recovered and broke through to every heart in that room. There's no way I can transcribe all the powerful words she said in those minutes, they were so meaningful and mature for someone who on certain days, I still view as so young, or maybe it's just in my mind's eye...wishing she was.

She had words of gratitude for so many, her tutor, her aunts and uncle, our neighbors, (who we consider our other family), her grandparents, cousins, myself, her mother Debbie and her sister, Emily. But maybe the most powerful words were the ones she wrote, but felt so strongly in the depths of her heart, she was unable to say out loud. Her tutor Lucia stepped up and stood by her side, to read what Sophie had written about her grandfather, her Poppy, who left us too soon, when Sophie was only nine years old:

"Poppy, here I am. It's my big day. The night I wrote this, I came downstairs crying to my Mom about how I didn't remember you enough. I remember you cooking us eggs, lox and onions in the morning. I remember the feeling of your prickly beard. I remember you sitting by the ocean while we collected seashells. But I think the only thing I need to remember is how much you loved us, and still do."

From a young heart still stinging from the pain of loss for one she loved so much. Sophie recovered and was able to continue on to talk about her little sister: "Emily, I think you are so beautiful and the most energetic person I've ever met and you're always smiling. You inspire me to look on the bright side of even the worst situations. I love you."

To me: "Daddy, I think you are the most amazing man I have ever met, you're so determined and hard-working and you are the person who taught me to never give up, which I think is the best thing a person could learn. I love you."

To Debbie: "Mommy, I have no clue what I would do without you. You help me through every possible problem I could ever have. Even though you nose your way into every dramatic issue I have, you always help me out in the end. You are the strongest person I have ever met, knowing what you have been through. Thank you for working your butt off so I could have the best day of my life. I love you."

"Last but not least I'd like to thank Adonai (God). I don't know how it worked out, but you made me an amazing life. I am so blessed with all of these amazing people. Thank you for being the one thing that can never leave my heart. Amen."

It was powerful and heartfelt and I held back my emotions the whole time, for fear of Sophie Rose looking down at me in the front row and seeing tears streaming down my face, only making it tougher for her. The tears are here now, hard to write and then read Sophie's words without it happening.

But there's one thing I need to correct about what she said about Debbie and I. There's a line I omitted from Sophie's speech about us: "I think I have the best parents ever and I'd like to thank them for everything."

The problem is my girl has got it all backward. It's we, who are grateful to her, for becoming the person she is today. Just maybe we are doing something right along the way. These miracles don't come with manuals, and it's Sophie, who has to take what she learns, and make it her own. From what I saw last night, she's on her way.

I've been talking about it for months now. Gratitude, appreciation and love. It's the hat trick and my beautiful daughter proved it, just ask anyone who was scrambling to find a tissue as she spoke, or sniffling their way through much of her ceremony. When you speak from the heart, everyone who has one, is all in.

I will leave you with this. Driving home this afternoon after a trip to the mall, the title of a song popped up on the screen of our satellite radio. It was a good one, a tune from a legend, Elton John. Before the lyrics began Debbie told Sophie to listen and to pay attention to the words and think about her ceremony.

The song? *Can You Feel the Love Tonight.*

Enough said.

Until next time, thanks for taking the time.

The Sunday Series: Heartlight

While I have previously felt the power of sharing our story, having shared our story with Mark and having him turn it into a Sunday Series piece to share with others has been an amazing experience. Mark was able to take our voice and share it in a way that reached a broader audience and affected others in a way that we had not previously been able to do. He intertwined my words with his and wove a beautiful tapestry that made even me feel as if I were hearing our story for the first time. Giving hope to even just one person is why we do this. It is why we share. It is why stories are told. It is precisely why I feel so fortunate to have had Mark share our story.

–Ali Lazorchak

You could literally see his heart beating. Hayden lay there, his chest wide open, covered only with some light bandages, in critical condition. His parents sitting by his bedside throughout the night, with one single purpose, one single desire, one single prayer...please let Hayden live.

It was only a little more than four years before that moment Hayden Lazorchak was born, prematurely. But at 4-lbs, 12-ounces, he was a seemingly healthy preemie, at least for a day. That's when doctors in the NICU discovered something was missing –half his heart. Hayden's issue was never caught in-utero. An ultrasound about halfway through the pregnancy showed all four chambers. But somewhere between that midpoint and his birth about a month earlier than normal, something failed to develop, and within 24 hours of his entry into this world the doctors knew Hayden would embark on a rare journey, one shrouded in a dark cloud of doubt that it could even succeed.

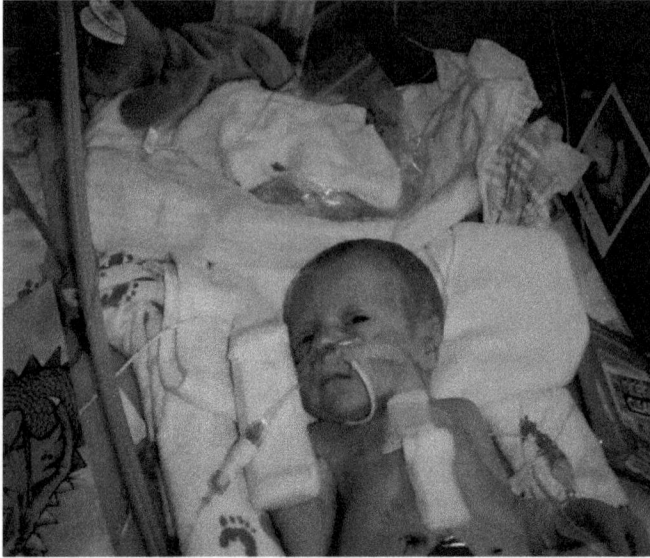

It's called Hypoplastic Left Heart Syndrome. HLHS is a rare congenital heart defect in which the left ventricle of the heart is severely underdeveloped, basically the person has only half a functioning heart. In babies with HLHS, the aorta and left ventricle are underdeveloped before birth, and the aortic and mitral valves are too small to allow sufficient blood flow. For Hayden, the doctors said his best chance at survival would be three corrective surgeries, the first to begin immediately, the second at six months, the third a few years down the road. That's the medical game plan. The reality is, no one could be sure it would work, but there was little choice.

So having entered the world only hours before, Hayden was about to undergo major open heart surgery. His parents, Ali and Rob were given time with their newborn son, to hold him, to take photos, to be in the moment, because at that moment, the doctors were unsure Hayden would even make it.

But somehow he did.

The first emergency surgery was deemed a success. Though Hayden spent a month in the hospital, he was then allowed to come home. Ali says the challenge of taking care of a new life, even a "normal" baby, can be overwhelming, but add to that the task of caring for a baby having undergone open heart surgery and the real challenge becomes creating as normal an existence as possible, especially when you know what is looming around the corner, surgery number two.

Ali says the first surgery was a "whirlwind," an immediate and necessary emergency procedure just to keep Hayden alive. But the second time around, Hayden was already six months old, "we knew him," says Ali, "this one was going to be so much harder."

And it was.

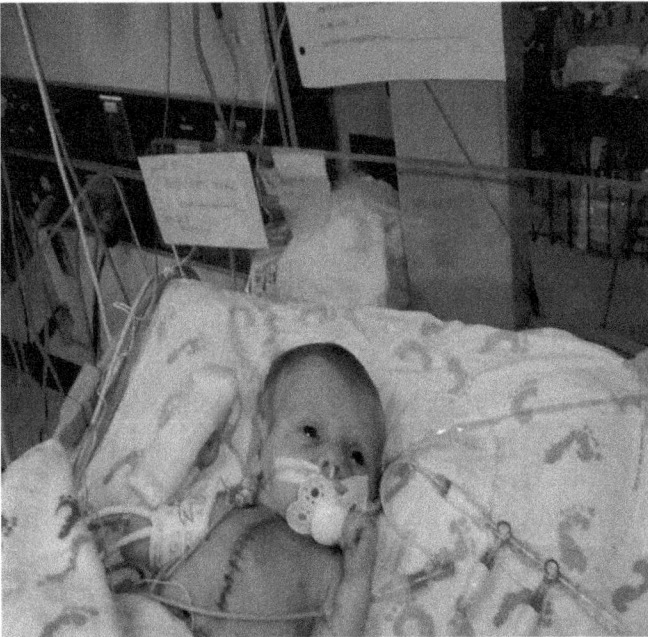

Hayden was supposed to be in the hospital for a week, his stay lasted four months. During that time, and through a myriad of complications, Hayden suffered, including becoming addicted to painkillers. This tiny life, a little more than half-a-year old, was now an addict, forced to be put on methadone to help wean him off the pain drugs which the doctors were forced to give Hayden just to help him exist. He had also been intubated for so long now, Hayden didn't even know how to eat on his own anymore. Physical and drug rehabilitation now became a part of this tiny baby's existence.

They say God does not give you more than you can handle. Sometimes that is hard to believe. During the same period, Ali was forced to undergo an emergency open appendectomy, after her appendix ruptured when she and Rob were out one evening. Ali says for her family, especially for Rob, with his son suffering, his wife recovering from her own major surgery, it seemed like the world was teetering on the brink. But Ali recovered and then Hayden, still less than one-year-old, having survived his second surgery and his "rehabilitation," eventually came home.

Except for the medications Hayden needed to take daily, Ali says life was, "really normal. We did everything normal families do." They did, but the Lazorchak's were doing even more. During Hayden's second surgery stay, Ali and Rob decided they needed to give back and created a non-profit organization called Hayden's Heart Heroes, with funds raised going directly to the pediatric cardiology division and the PICU at Johns Hopkins Hospital, where Hayden was being treated. Ali says when you are going through something like this there are "two roads to take. Get through it and then try to forget it, or do something about it. For us, it was about doing and emotionally that's where we were able to put our energy, it gave us direction." (http://www.haydensheartheroes.com/)

For the next few years, the direction for the Lazorchak family was a positive one. Outside of the visits with their cardiologist Dr. Joel Brenner, and the daily medications, Hayden was living and growing just like a normal child. Ali says from the outside, it was impossible to tell he had been through so much. That's what made surgery number three, the final one the doctors told them about shortly after Hayden was born, so tough to take. "It was horrible for us," says Ali, "unbelievably difficult because he was totally this little person. You already have all these connections. He loved to sing, loved to golf, it was so much different than when he was a baby, at four-years-old, it was so much more real and it was very hard to hand him over that day."

Hard quickly became an understatement. The prior surgeries had not been easy, this one ended up requiring a heart-lung bypass and the discovery of a tricuspid valve leakage. On the surgery table for ten hours, the doctors would come out to give updates to Ali and Rob, and none of them were positive. The doctors believed by that evening, Hayden might need to go on full life support. Coming out of surgery that day Hayden's chest remained open because of a build-up of fluid, the doctors pumped him with diuretics for three full days. The rabbi who came to see Hayden nearly fainted when he saw the young boy lying there with his chest open, his heart visibly beating.

But in nothing short of a miracle the doctors were able to stabilize the young boy. They closed him up and after overcoming a few more complications, discussion of a heart transplant, which Ali and Rob somehow convinced the doctors would not be needed, and more than a month in the hospital, Hayden finally came home.

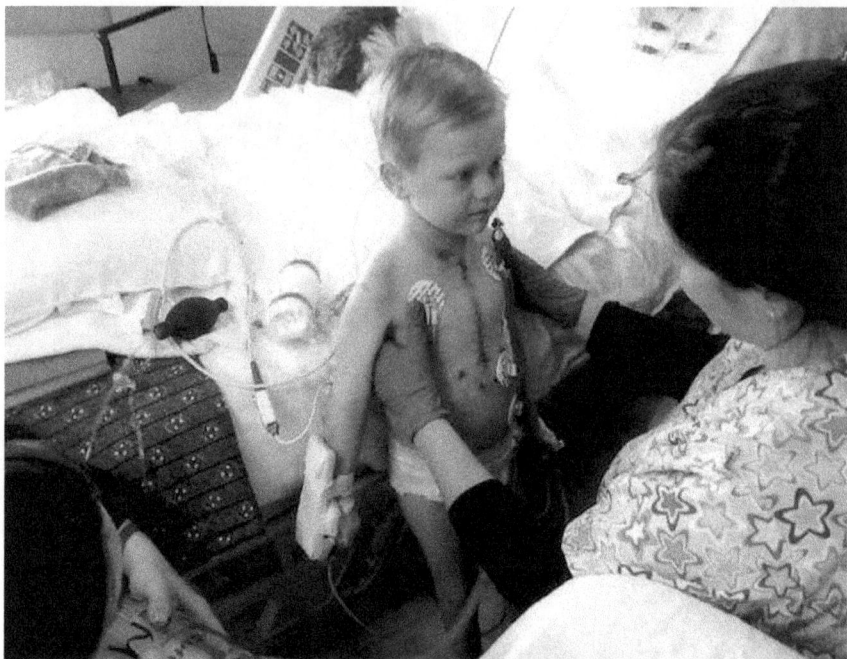

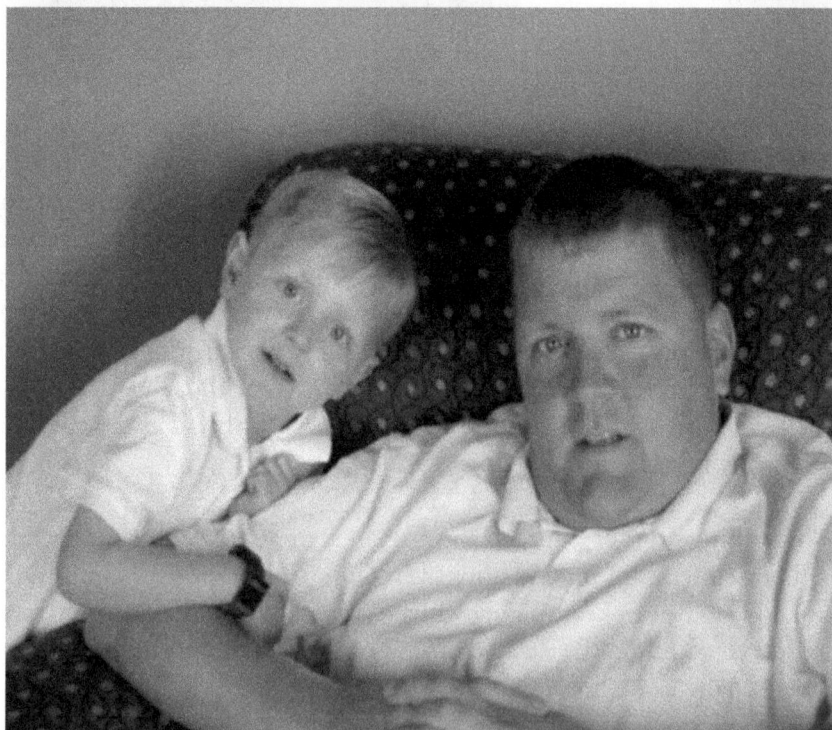

Hayden is now 9-years old and slowly over these past five years his heart function has steadily improved, his valve leakage is no longer an issue and doctors say his heart is the best it has ever been. Hayden takes a daily dose of the blood thinner Cumadin, which he will do for the rest of his life, but Ali says to him all of this is normal. She and Rob have fought hard to make life normal for Hayden and for them and to continue to give back. Hayden's Heart Heroes will hold its 9th golf tournament this June and the book fair this fall, and the foundation is about to hit the $100,000 mark in donations.

In the end, it's all about heart. Whether it's a half, a whole, or something in between. It's not the heart muscle, but the light which emanates from its core, and touches all those who come in contact. For Ali and Rob, it's the glow of that light, Hayden's light, now stronger than ever, which makes their own hearts shine ever brighter.

Until next time, thanks for taking the time.

The Sunday Series: The Breath of Life

If you have ever been pregnant, or loved someone that was carrying a baby, you can imagine the state of desperation and distress that I was in. I wanted this my entire life, the gift of being a mom. And now it was dangled in front of me... you or the baby.

–Ashley Silcott

Life isn't fair. But you hope you get the chance in life to wage a fair fight. Have a goal, make a plan, take a deep breath and take action. But what if breath won't come easy, what if oxygen is hard to come by, what do you do when good air is rare? You try your best to breathe...or maybe hold that breath and wait for a miracle.

Sometimes miracles happen. For Ashley Silcott, this is life. Breathing life into the future, to future plans, for the chance to make it day-to-day always seems to hang in the balance. Ashley has Cystic Fibrosis, (CF). It is a chronic, progressive and frequently fatal (genetic) inherited disease, primarily affecting the respiratory and digestive system. For much of Ashley's time on this planet, the hospital has become a second home. She's been admitted more than 50 times, to get breathing treatments, medication, IV's, and more.

Ashley was diagnosed with CF at birth. She says, "one day I feel great, the next I can barely function. I take over thirty pills a day and spend hours doing breathing treatments and physical therapy regimens just to try and stay healthy." And then there's this constant cough. The one Ashley says she's had her whole life. The cough which led other kids to make fun of her in school, the cough which make other people think she's contagious. The one that won't ever go away.

The average life expectancy of someone living with Cystic Fibrosis...37. A little more than a decade from where 25 year old Ashley is now in her life. But Ashley's not average, she is determined to help change that number, to beat that "average." One way to do it is to fight, the other, most unexpectedly for Ashley, is to become immortal. But immortality comes with a price. Ashley nearly paid with her life.

In January of 2013, Ashley was back at Johns Hopkins Hospital where she had been so many times for breathing treatments, to help fight off infection, to help her simply keep going. She had never stayed for more than 10 days, but this time the journey would be much, much longer. This time life would hang in the balance and that balancing act would affect more than just one life.

During this hospital stay, Ashley wasn't responding to treatment. Things were going downhill...and fast. "Each day, my symptoms worsened," Ashley says. "I was eventually moved to a critical care floor where my resting heart rate resembled that of someone who had been working out vigorously for hours. I had high fevers, 103, 104...for hours each day. My body was in overdrive just trying to keep me alive. My kidneys began to fail. I was coughing up blood and throwing up hourly. I eventually lost control of my bladder and I could no longer walk because I was so weak. My body would collapse merely trying to stand. I was in such terrible, constant pain and agony that all I could think was, "this is it, this is the end. This is how twenty-four years of fighting is going to end. I was utterly terrified. I'll remember the entire, horrible, terrifying experience for the rest of my life. Laying in the critical care bed, with my mom and dad, my husband Tyler and my cousin Abby beside me – I knew. I could feel it."

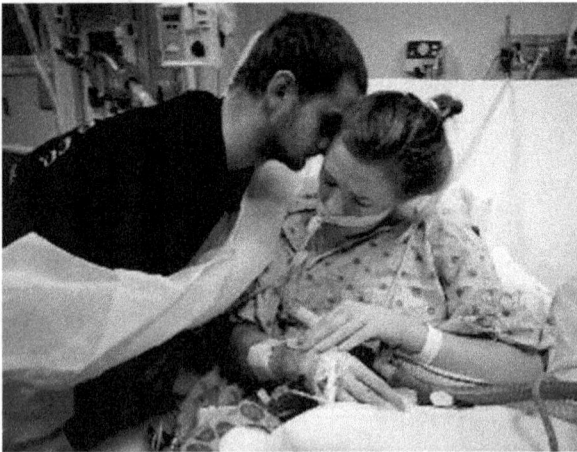

And what Ashley could feel was more than a health crisis, it was despair. Because what she and Tyler had kept from the rest of the family was a secret, one they had, pre-hospital stay, gone to great lengths to research, to speak to the experts and talk about to each other, so they could tell their family the news with joy in their eyes and not fear in their hearts. Ashley was pregnant. It wasn't planned, but it was reality and once it happened Ashley and Tyler were determined to bring this miracle of life to life.

But as she got sicker and sicker and a decision was made to move her to the Intensive Care Unit (ICU), the treatment plan Ashley had been approving or disapproving, for fear it would affect her fetus, gave it all away. Finally, her Dad overheard her conversation with the doctors, and Ashley broke down in tears as she admitted to her father she was with child. "My Dad took a long walk at that point," Ashley says, "then came back and was more supportive than she could have imagined. My Mom was terrified, but supportive." Yet now that it was out in the open, the life-changing decisions were getting tougher.

"If you have ever been pregnant, or loved someone that was carrying a baby, you can imagine the state of desperation and distress that I was in," says Ashley. "I wanted this my entire life, the gift of being a mom. And now it was dangled in front of me. "You or the baby." I chose both. There's no question. For me there was no OR. It was then that I found out who my true loved ones were. Those that loved me accepted my decision to fight for BOTH of us, not just one. Others considered me selfish and foolish. Either way, I had made up my mind."

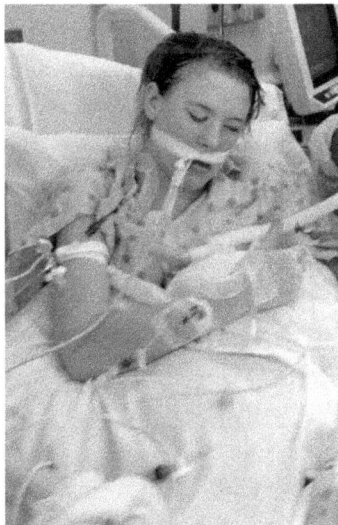

But what you decide and what life decides to place in your path are often not on the same page. Things had gotten bad. Ashley was refusing treatments which could help her, but hurt the baby. And now she was no longer breathing on her own, on a ventilator, sedated and basically in a medically-induced coma, it was Ashley's Dad, to whom she had given medical power of attorney, who made the decision for treatments to save her life. But the ventilator was no longer helping Ashley to breathe and the doctors and the family agreed a tracheostomy (trache) would be necessary. They woke Ashley to tell her what would happen next.

Ashley still remembers what it felt like after she learned the news, knowing the procedure would happen the next day, if not sooner: "I knew this day would come. Everything I've ever read, heard or witnessed about Cystic Fibrosis proved that. CF is a vicious monster that doesn't stop. It's unpredictable. Perfectly healthy 50-year-olds are living with CF over here. And a three-year-old is dying because of it over there. Unpredictable. CF does not discriminate. And it is downright cruel. And that's how I went to sleep. Convinced that I would die right there that very night in my sleep. Heartbroken. Silent. Defeated."

Ashley continues, "I drifted off to the most panicked, restless sleep of my life. My hand on my precious stomach, praying to whoever was listening. Pleading and begging for another chance. Because apparently that's what you do when you're dying, you cling to life like never before. And I was literally, clinging to life. I held my stomach, somehow hoping that this little person inside me could feel that I loved them.. I just hoped that he or she knew that I tried. And off to sleep we went. Surely to meet angels tonight. Or so I thought."

But that night's prayers were answered...sometimes, miracles happen.

"I woke up and couldn't believe I was alive," says Ashley. "My mom and the respiratory therapist came in and told me I had been breathing on my own for an hour. They took the ventilator out and I started talking, slowly at first. Progress, progress throughout the day. I had not stood up in a month. I had lost more than 20 pounds. I was just so small. No muscle mass, no fat. In an insanely short amount of time, about two weeks, I was out of the hospital."

By Valentine's Day, the baby, "popped," meaning Ashley now had the pregnancy belly. She says she gained about 10 pounds nearly overnight.

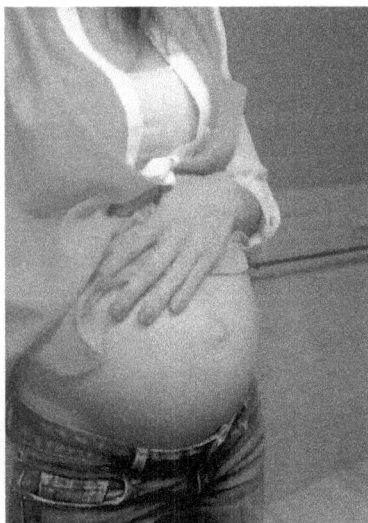

Pregnancy was tough, because Ashley was still doing rehab and needed help with walking and was incredibly anxious about the health of the baby, calling the doctor at least twice a day every time she thought the baby had stopped moving.

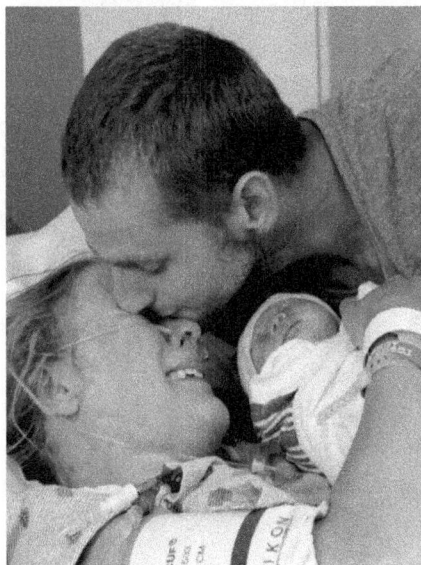

But on June 26th, life moved forward in a way which has changed Ashley's life. Despite coming six weeks early, Preslee, at 6-pounds, 10-ounces, was born. Healthy, with no signs the little girl had endured any stress, Preslee was perfect.

This was the breath of life Ashley and Tyler had been waiting for. "She (Preslee), has made me fight one-thousand times harder than I ever thought I could," says Ashley. I'm coming up on one-year-hospital-free.

That has never happened. She just keeps me going. I don't have time to rest, or to get sick. She's the reason I take my medicine, the reason I get up every day. I no longer think about being sick. It no longer has power over me. The love I have for her is stronger than any medicine out there."

For Ashley the fight isn't over, it never will be until she says the letters, CF, which stand for Cystic Fibrosis, can stand for Cure Found. You can help. Learn more or donate at, http://fightcf.cff.org/goto/ashleysarmy

I asked Ashley what one thing she thinks she can share to inspire others from her experience. She said it's one word...**hope.** "I think I never let go of hope, because hope prevails. It can be tough, but it's worth holding onto. If you're not positive, if you let yourself go to a dark place, it won't work. I think it's staying positive. I thought positive throughout the entire experience and it brought me to where I am today. It has made me a stronger and more motivated person. Whatever you are going through in life, I think you have to have hope you can get to a better place."

It's hope and maybe just a little inspiration, a breath of fresh air, the breath of life, from a little girl named Preslee.

Until next time, thanks for taking the time.

The Sunday Series: Wheels of Giving

I was so happy to have Mark tell my story of all the good work I do for the National MS Society. Letting everyone know where the dollars I have raised for MS have gone and letting everyone know that our money is really making a difference. In my story, we were able to bring more awareness about MS to the community and I can't thank Mark enough.

—Jill Eisenberg

Ten years, thousands of miles, and to think it all began one day at lunch.

"There's a group at my office, (GP Strategies), that rides," says Jill Eisenberg, "and I had not been on a bike since age 12 or 13. My co-workers ride at lunchtime, I just started riding with them." And once the wheels started turning, Jill learned she couldn't be stopped. Working as a graphic designer, Jill quickly learned that riding became a great way to break up the day. "It's fun to put in saddle time," says Jill. "Lunchtime is usually 12-15 miles. Bike riding is extremely relaxing, by myself or with a group, it's a great way to clear my head. Sometimes someone might ask me for an idea and I go out and ride and think about it."

The daily rides got Jill thinking about bigger and better things, about challenging herself to do more, ride more, farther, faster and break through barriers. She did several bigger rides, including a 100-mile ride with a team from work, in an event called Seagull Century. Then Jill learned about a ride for Multiple Sclerosis. 100-miles one day, 50-miles the next through Maryland's beautiful eastern shore. At first, Jill saw the event and the ride as simply another challenge to take on, a shot at proving to herself she had the stamina and discipline to get it done. But as she learned more about MS and met some of the participants, everything changed.

Multiple Sclerosis, commonly referred to as MS, is a disease that affects the central nervous system, (CNS), and everything we do relies on the proper function of this central nervous system. But with MS, immune cells violate the connections of the CNS creating dysfunction, which can be mild, moderate or severe. There is no cure, only treatment...but events like Bike MS, are going a long way to improve those treatments, with people like Jill and thousands of others leading the charge.

(http://www.nationalmssociety.org/What-is-MS/Definition-of-MS)

And it was on one of these rides about four years ago that Jill met Mike. Mike was diagnosed with MS in his early 30's and was taking part in Bike MS. Jill was on the 100-mile route of the race when she came upon Mike. The two started talking and Jill realized he would need some encouragement to make it to the finish line, for the race leg he had chosen was not the 100-mile course, but a 65-mile trek. Jill stayed with Mike for every pedal the rest of the way and Mike told Jill his whole story of dealing with the disease. The two finished the 65-mile race together, and a new friendship blossomed.

Inspired by Jill and her dedication to cycling, the next year Mike said he wanted to tackle the 100-mile ride. The temperature for the ride that year, at 95 degrees, presented a significant challenge to both of them, especially Mike. Jill says every 10-miles she would ask him how he felt. Despite the heat and fatigue, Mike said he could make it. Slowly, methodically, the two pedaled together and reached the finish line, one of the final participants to cross, but it hardly mattered, a major obstacle had been overcome. And every year since then Mike has finished the 100-mile course.

Events like the Bike MS are literally changing the lives of those battling the disease. Over the past decade, Jill says she has witnessed tremendous strides in the research and treatments, some of it funded with the money raised by events like Bike MS. "The money we raise in Maryland is really doing great things," says Jill. "In the last ten years, the (treatments) have gone from daily shots to oral medications, so the person with MS can now take a pill with fewer side effects. MS affects things we don't think about, that we take for granted and the money raised is also funding more research, funding services for people who need assistance, ride shares, new beds and more." The drugs to treat MS can be expensive and not all is covered by insurance, events like Bike MS seek to alleviate the financial burden as well.

And Jill is a leader among those raising dollars to fight for those afflicted. Over the past ten years, Jill and her team, which now stands at 35 participants, have raised more than $20,000. In 2011, Jill was named Volunteer of the Year for the Maryland MS Chapter. It's all about going above and beyond what is expected, put the extra in front of ordinary to become extraordinary. Jill has found a cause she loves and does so by pouring her heart into it every year. "I know that I am extremely fortunate," says Jill. "I have good health, a healthy family, and because I'm healthy and I am able to give back, I should."

It takes each of us to make a difference for all of us. Jill Eisenberg is earning this first-hand as she and so many others help in the fight to create this world...a world free of MS and a world which is better because of those called to rise and make change happen. For Mike and countless others like him, more than 100,000 riders are changing lives and transforming their own. Jill trains, riding a few times a week at lunch and longer rides on the weekends, just to prepare for the bigger races like Bike MS. It's dedication and discipline. Taking small consistent steps to enact massive change. It's an example for all of us to follow. Find your passion, what you love to do and use your ability and talent to change the lives of other people. This is the essence of significance. You can play a significant part for Jill's team as well, if you would like to donate, or even join the team, go to (http://main.nationalmssociety.org/goto/TeamDesignConnection) or

(http://main.nationalmssociety.org/goto/jilleisenberg). And to think how great change began with a simple break for lunch. A lunchtime ride, which turned into the ride of a lifetime.

Until next time, thanks for taking the time.

The Sunday Series: Believe Big

"Thank you Mark for the work you do writing The Sunday Series. As someone who works with cancer patients who battle fear and anxiety each day, the need for hope and encouragement is essential. Your stories do just that! Thank you for sharing the stories that could have been missed and now are shared to inspire us to be all that God created us to be."

Her name is Ivelisse Page. And though her beautiful name begins with an "I", she knows there is no "I" in team. Every dream needs a team. It can't exist without one. Ivelisse could teach a lesson in Reach your Dream 101. And you might just say it is her destiny....

"I'm going to share one story I rarely share. My closest friends didn't know about this. The summer after my father's death, (Ivelisse's father died of colon cancer when she was 13), I went to summer camp with my youth group and there was a guest preacher there. He prayed and told me that God told him I was going to play an integral role in finding a cure for cancer. I was 13. I was intrigued. I asked around at camp if anyone mentioned anything to the preacher about my Dad, the cancer or anything else. Everyone said no. For many years I didn't tell anyone this story, not even my mom. As the years passed, I thought the guy had made a mistake. But 24 years later...."

There was no mistake. In September of 2008 Ivelisse started on the path toward her destiny, but what she didn't know was she wouldn't be drawn to destiny, it would literally pass right through her. First stop, cancer.

"My father died just two years after being diagnosed with colon cancer. I was diagnosed the same age as my father, at 37, but I had taken precautions. My father's mother and half of her siblings had colon cancer and all died from it. I was taking all the precautions, eating organic foods, exercising and getting colonoscopies every five years." What Ivelisse knows now, but didn't know at that time, is a small tumor can go from polyp to cancer in 36 months. "If here is a strong genetic link you should be tested every year, not every five," says Ivelisse. And it can come without warning.

"I had no symptoms besides being tired. I was taking two-to-three hour naps every day. Raising four kids, I thought I was just a tired, busy mom. My husband finally said this is just not right, something is really wrong. So I made an appointment with the doctor and he said, "you are severely anemic, you need to go to the ER...right now...and get a blood transfusion. I had no one there at the moment to help me. My husband and my mom were out of town. I told the doctor, I have my kids at home, what am I going to do?" At the same time, Jimmy, her husband was in an airport in Georgia about to board a plane to California, but when Ivelisse called Jimmy looked up to see there was another flight to Baltimore. He ran to the ticket counter and told them they must switch his flight, the airline honored his request and within 90 minutes he was home.

But the journey was just beginning.

The doctor couldn't figure out why Ivelisse was so anemic. He said there was no reason for it to be a colon issue, Ivelisse had just had a colonoscopy three years prior...but they elected to do another one. The colonoscopy revealed cancer in the colon, it was in the lymph nodes, stage-3. Sometimes three is a magic number, to Ivelisse it didn't feel that way, but by doing the colonoscopy at that time, that single test probably saved her life. "At that moment I did cry," says Ivelisse. "Your life flashes before you, you have this diagnosis and knowing what my father and his family went through...you try to overcome the fear trying to grip you. But when I got home, I had to make a decision. Am I going to live by fear, or by faith and fight? I made the choice I'm going to live by faith and fight, and that's what I held on to."

Ivelisse and Jimmy had the difficult conversation with their four children. Her oldest, who had done some research on the internet about colon cancer, asked his mom if she was going to die. Ivelisse told her son, "none of us knows what tomorrow will bring, if we are here, or not. I know things don't look good when you go online and read, but God is good no matter what and I will fight as hard as I can to be here. Stay off the internet and fill your mind with things which are encouraging, not discouraging." The surgery to remove the cancer was a success and only 1-of-28 lymph nodes was affected, still, it was recommended Ivelisse see an oncologist for follow-up. "Surely," Ivelisse says, "with all the years since my father had passed, there must be advancements which give me a better chance of surviving. We interviewed several oncologists and found Dr. Diaz at Johns Hopkins Hospital. But when we asked Dr. Diaz about my chances of surviving with chemotherapy, he told us at that point, it was a 67% survival rate, without chemo it was 57%. It only improved my chances by 10%...my husband and I looked at each other and decided we were not going to do it." But as more testing was done it was discovered that the cancer had spread to the liver, Ivelisse was now stage-4. Devastating. Her chances of survival this time around, only 8%. Chemo wouldn't change a thing.

During this period, Ivelisse and Jimmy started looking around for alternatives. There had to be a better way, a better shot at survival. They learned about mistletoe therapy. Mistletoe, the same plant which garners all the attention at holiday time bringing people together, sometimes in the tradition of a single kiss underneath the greenery. Ivelisse and Jimmy hoped this time mistletoe might help kiss cancer goodbye. The couple was introduced to Dr. Peter Hinderberger, who handles anthroposophic (alternative) medicine. He taught them about the healing effects of mistletoe, which attacks the bad cancer cells, but leaves the good ones intact. Through research, Ivelisse and Jimmy learned mistletoe can also stimulate bone marrow activity, help ease tumor-related pain and reduce the risk of reoccurrence of cancer. And it could be used right alongside chemotherapy to help reduce the side effects of chemo. 60% of cancer patients in Europe are on mistletoe therapy.

Ivelisse was sold and two weeks prior to the liver surgery she began mistletoe therapy treatments. During the surgery, 20% of her liver was dissected, but the margins were clear. Ivelisse went in for post-op and another scan. Before the doctor gave the results, she and Jimmy asked him what were the chances of something showing up again. The doctor asked her, "do you really want to know?" The couple said they did and the doctor told her, 75% of the time they find more tumor activity. Ivelisse says her husband Jimmy looked over at her and told her, "you are going to be part of that 25%."

That was more than five years ago. Miracles happen and Ivelisse is living one. At the three-year mark of being cancer-free, Dr. Diaz told Ivelisse, this is "monumental" to be part of the 8% who survive stage-IV colon cancer. And that was when This survivor told the doctor she wanted to do more to share her mistletoe treatment story. She wanted to raise money to fund clinical trials, but as Dr. Diaz explained to her, not only would it be a daunting task, but there was another challenge, no pharmaceutical company could touch it because mistletoe is a natural substance, so funds must be raised privately.

Words like daunting, challenge, and the like mean little when you have the belief, you carry the faith and find your purpose. Ivelisse knew then she had to dream big, live big, believe big. It had been nearly a quarter-century since a preacher at summer camp told Ivelisse she would "play in integral role in finding a cure for cancer," and in April of 2011, Believe Big was born. It began simply with Believe Big mugs, handed out to patients at the oncology center while Ivelisse waited for her appointments. But since that time, so much more has happened.

Through different events and Ivelisse and Jimmy's dedication to the cause, Believe Big has raised $300,000 and Phase 1 of the clinical trials on mistletoe therapy is underway. Phases 2 and 3 will take millions to fund and years to complete, but the energy is there and the cause is worth it. Ivelisse says, "the good thing is mistletoe therapy is available now and there are 50 physicians trained across the United States to administer it with treatments.

Though not covered by insurance, the treatments cost only about $100-$150 a month. Believe Big even has grant dollars available to help patients with the cost of the treatments. At the most recent Believe Big dinner, just last month, the non-profit foundation raised more than $196,000. The theme? 'Kissing Cancer Goodbye.'

"My why and my passion for doing what I do each day," says Ivelisse, "is because I don't want anyone else to lose their mom, dad, brother, or sister. I want people to know there are complimentary things out there to help fight cancer and to bridge the gap between conventional medicine and other treatments. We want to cure the whole person, to use the strength of both practices and let people know there are other things out there to help heal. Even creating the website, (http://www.believebig.org/), as a place for people to go as a guide for what to look for, we don't want it to be difficult for anyone to find the information. You are going through a hurricane of emotions, (when cancer is diagnosed), and so we created Believe Big, so there's one place to go, one resource for patients to advocate for their own health.

Face it. Fight it. Overcome it. Those are the three sentences on the foundation's website. Sometimes three is a magic number. Ivelisse and her family are making magic and more.

Want to change the world? Just ask Ivelisse Page...sometimes you just have to Believe Big.

Until next time, thanks for taking the time.

The Sunday Series: Unconditional

Until Mark wrote our family's story I never shared anything about my daughter Cassie, who has very severe autism. Maybe I was afraid people wouldn't understand. Maybe I was afraid of people's responses – possible rejection. Whatever the reason, Mark explained about my daughter in a way that made people able to know her – able to understand who she is, the struggle she encounters daily, and how much she is worthy of being loved for who she is. Since Mark told our story, I am no longer private – I don't have reason to be anymore because now that people understand, the community has embraced her. This has given me the courage and strength to share all aspects of our lives. I now network with families going through similar challenges. I have participated in organizing fundraisers on Cassie's behalf, to raise money for her school, and so much more. The careful, loving way Mark presented our story, has truly changed our lives… and opened the world up to us!

–Jennifer Drucker

So you wish upon a star, sometimes lots of stars, the sun, the moon, the deep blue sky, praying for your dream to come true. But the dream doesn't always work out the way you want. It might be different than you imagined, not exactly what you envisioned, but it doesn't mean your life remains unchanged or transformed. In fact, you might just become the person you never expected to be. Or maybe you find the kind of love you never knew existed.

It's pretty simple. All Jennifer Drucker wanted out of her adult life was to have a daughter. She had saved everything from her childhood: her stuffed animals, her stationary collection, her sticker collection, her comic books, and all the things she loved as a teenager, just so she could pass them on to her little girl. All she wanted was that perfect little girl.

Jennifer and her husband Frank BonGiorno were living in a townhouse community in Long Island, New York when their little girl, Cassie, entered the world.

The changes were slow at first.

Jen had a friend who also had a daughter about five months older than Cassie. Jen noticed the other girl seemed to be developing faster than her own daughter. Her friend noticed it as well, but kept quiet for some time. Jen said Cassie could crawl before she could even turn over. And then there was the fascination with a certain toy. "Remember those toys that made noise and had little dots that formed the speaker?" says Jen, "Cassie would sit with the toy and bang her knuckles on those speaker dots over and over and over, lost in her own little world. She would bang so long and so hard callouses formed on her knuckles." Jen's friends jokingly referred to Cassie as a "knuckle-holic." But for Jen it was no joke, she felt something was wrong.

At ten months, Jen took Cassie to the doctor and told them something isn't right, the doctor didn't agree with Jen and said everything was fine, don't worry. At the one year check-up, Jen told the doctor about some of the odd behaviors. The doctor said she was panicking for no reason, Cassie was developing, all kids do different things. But not two weeks later Jen brought Cassie back to the doctor. And this time Jen was hysterical, she demanded her daughter be tested, something wasn't right. The doctors ran some tests and gave Jen and Frank the diagnosis...autism.

Within days Cassie was in a day-long early intervention program for autistic children. Help was coming to the home as well, speech, occupational and physical therapy services and a ton of special education hours. The changes continued. At 14 months, Cassie started walking...within 48 hours she was running. Jen says, "kids with autism, their skills are so splintered, they can be so advanced in one area and so behind in another. If you've got one child with autism, you've got one child with autism...no two are alike. If there are six autistic children in a room, there need to be seven adults, because each child's behavior is different and they must have individualized attention. What's also commonly diagnosed with autism is Tourette's Syndrome, ADHD and sometimes intellectual disability. Sometimes they say with autism, it's in there, (the knowledge), but they just can't get it out. It's not in there with Cassie."

Jen continues, "Cassie knows shapes, colors, addresses...anything she can memorize she knows. But she doesn't understand anything abstract. When she's present she is so sweet and cute, she asks for tickles and 'chase me.' But then she has her self-stimulatory behaviors. When a kid has autism, they want to present themselves through something, like a stick, to touch other objects. For Cassie it's the straps of a plastic bucket, you know those white handles of the bucket and shovel kits you get as a kid? This is Cassie's whole life. Not the bucket and shovel, just the white strap."

And Cassie has to have that strap. There is no telling her it doesn't exist, no substitution. Jen says they finally convinced this company to send them one-thousand bucket handles, just the handles, (at 7 cents apiece). "Cassie bends the strap, and shakes it and that's when you know you she's lost in her world of autism," says Jen. "She will tell me, "I need a break" and go off in her world." Without that strap Jen says Cassie would melt down and never be able to stop asking for it. She has to have that strap.

To speak to Jen Drucker is to understand courage in the face of adversity. She is handling her day-to-day challenges with her daughter the best she can. And those challenges are many.

Like the time they ran out of food, Cassie's food. Cassie will only eat four foods and one of those are gluten-free, casein-free (lactose-free) chicken nuggets from a specific company. Cassie, who is now 14, has been eating those nuggets three-times-a-day for the past 12-1/2 years. A little while back the company that makes the nuggets had to shut down for six months and it led to one of the greatest challenges Jen had to face. Without those nuggets, Cassie refused to eat, she would starve. This little girl with autism couldn't comprehend what was going on, she couldn't be told there were no nuggets. There couldn't be any substitution. She might starve to death. The company worked with the family and found stores all over the country that still had the nuggets on their shelves and family and friends helped to gather them up and put them in storage. But with four days to go before production was to begin again, Jen ran out of nuggets. Cassie didn't eat for four days. She only drank juice, she was so upset and stressed over the situation she simply stopped eating.

Jen says Cassie is such a creature of routine and since she was a little girl, Jen has fed her. Even at 14, she still wants and needs Jen to feed her, to bathe her, to dress her, to do other things most of us take for granted. Then there are the medications Cassie must take for anxiety. Jen says, "every time we leave the house, Cassie is stressed, except for going to school. She has no idea where she is going. She doesn't know if it's for something fun, or to go have surgery."

Cassie had major surgery at the tender age of five, when her lung collapsed and no one knew it. Jen says children with autism can't always show pain, or even explain it, so they had no idea, until it was almost too late. Cassie spent four weeks in the hospital, but it was after surgery that Jen says she experienced one of the highs in her life, when her 5-year-old, who was almost completely non-verbal, said the word which melted Jen's heart..."mommy.'

Living in the world of autism can be a challenge for any family and Jen says for her and Frank it was no different. Their marriage ended in divorce. It's been four years now that Jen has been a single mom, moving back to Maryland, where she grew up and is now living amongst her greatest support system, her childhood friends. Those same friends who last year organized a fundraiser for Cassie's school, raising nearly $5,000.

Cassie has a great friend too, her brother, Sam. Sam is two years younger than Cassie and was, as Jen describes, a "9-11 baby." The family was still living just outside New York, when the terrorist strikes ravaged the city and rocked the world. Cassie was at her special school, which when the planes hit the buildings, went into lockdown. Jen and Frank couldn't get to Cassie, and it was then Jen became petrified of what would happen if something happened to her and Frank. Cassie would be all alone in the world. Sam is the product of that fear, but it was meant to be, because he's also now

Cassie's guardian angel. Jen says Sam knows everything about Cassie, he is so great with her. "Cassie is the sweetest person I have ever met," says Jen, "but Sam might be sweeter. We live in a court with more than a dozen kids and they will come knocking on the door to ask Sam to play, but if Sam is doing something with Cassie, he will put them off, telling them he'll be there soon, after he's finished playing with his sister."

But Sam's life is also a by-product of Jen's constant attention to and responsibility for Cassie. "Sam is the kid at his sporting event without a parent there," says Jen. "It's difficult and expensive for me to spend time alone with him." Jen has to pay a babysitter, (one who she can trust with Cassie), plus the cost of whatever activity she and Sam might do, like going to a movie, and getting a snack. Even the simple act of taking Sam alone to get a haircut is a challenge. And not to mention Jen's alone time. The time for her to experience adult life, void of the day-to-day challenges of being the mother of a child with autism. A mother's job is tough enough, the world's toughest, but the respite from that responsibility is not something Jen took advantage of for quite some time. "It took me a lot to learn balance," says Jen. "I gave my freedom away in my 30's, it was all Cassie and dealing with (family issues)." Now Jen goes out at least one night a week with her friends, to get a break and get recharged.

From speaking with Jen, there is story after story after story I could tell on this blog. Jen's description of her life with Cassie could be, should be, its own blog, its own journal. I asked Jen about the highs-and-lows of the past 14 years with Cassie. She says the high was when she heard the word "mommy" for that first time following Cassie's surgery. The low? It was the day the neurologist confirmed what her pediatrician had finally diagnosed – Cassie had autism. "I just wanted to die," says Jen. Everything she had saved for that someday, for the day she had a daughter, it no longer mattered. Jen knew she couldn't pass on any of those things, Cassie has no interest, she could care less.

Except what Cassie gives Jen every day goes far beyond worldly possessions. Jen says she is not the same person she was before Cassie, and when asked to describe the one thing she can share with others because of her experience of raising an autistic child, it's this: "There is value in every person. No matter who they are, how developed or not, every person has so much to offer us, if you just give them a chance and just pay attention. With Cassie, with everything that's not there, what I get back from being her mom is just amazing, because I allow that. When a child has been struggling for years and years and she achieves something, there's nothing like it. Don't judge. Just open up and you will grow. Cassie is such a special person and if you don't pay attention to the things that make her special, you'll miss it."

To the world you might be just one person, but to one person you might just be the world. For Cassie this is Jen. Sometimes you wish on a star, the sun, the moon, the deep blue sky, for a dream to come true. You wonder if Cassie could truly speak, if she could experience those abstract emotions and turn them into words, into sentences, what she might say to Jen.

I bet she'd tell her how the stars, the sun, the moon and the deep blue sky, for her, look like one perfect person. The person she calls, "mommy."

Until next time, thanks for taking the time.

The Sunday Series: From Sea to Shining Sea

I want to ride, ride like the wind, to be free again.

–Christopher Cross

"A lot of people consider our journey across the country almost like their fight against cancer. Knowing we are fighting right along with them gets them going, especially on the tougher days.

–Natalie Fischer

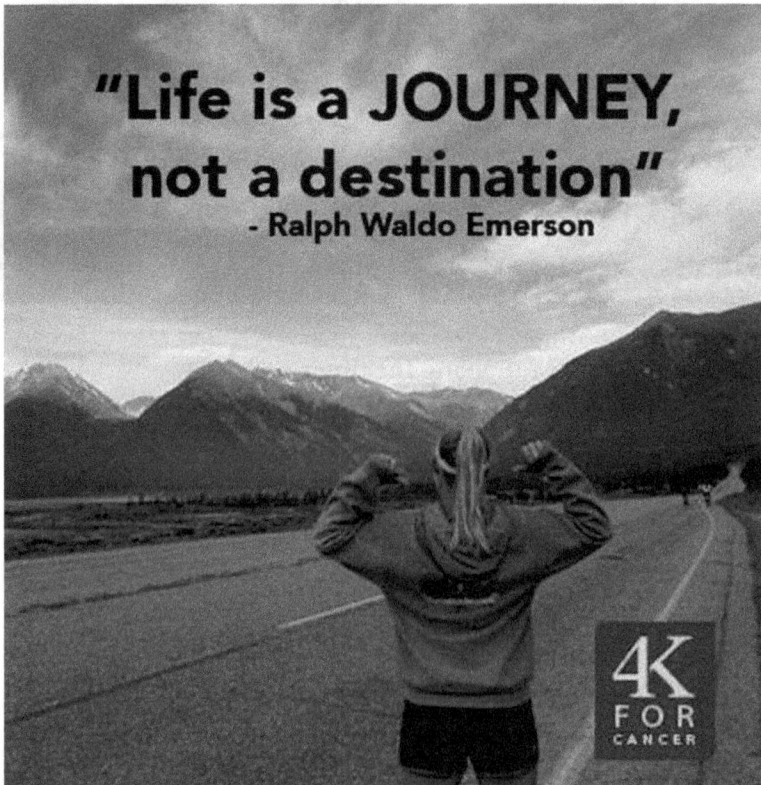

Those who can are doing it for those who can't. It started in early June and you can bet as you are reading this, their wheels are turning, as groups of college students are biking across America with the goal of offering support and funding for young cancer victims along the way. It is hope for the future and these kids are giving up their summer to do just that, bring hope to tomorrow, hope to those who sometimes feel as if there is none, those young adults fighting the big "C." It is inspiration at its finest. It is the 4K for Cancer, a four thousand mile ride to help in the battle against the beast.

The Ulman Cancer Fund for Young Adults was founded by Doug Ulman, who at the age of 19 was diagnosed with a cancerous tumor in his back and is now a three-time cancer survivor. As with so many great ideas, the Ulman Cancer Fund started with a simple discussion around the dining room table, as Doug, several family members, friends and neighbors dreamed up the plan for this organization to help young adults with cancer. Since 1997 the organization has been providing crucial support to thousands of young adults in need. The 4K for Cancer is one of its premiere events.

One of those making this year's ride is 22-year-old Natalie Fischer. Natalie and 24 other college-age students are part of Team Seattle, they are making the ride from Baltimore to the Great Northwest. They left on June 1st and as of this writing are in Chicago, as they pedal with a purpose across this great land, to their final destination in Seattle on August 9th. "There are a lot of different reasons I joined," says Natalie. "I enjoy biking, I've done triathlons before this and I've always dreamed about riding across the country. I interned at the Ulman Cancer Fund two summers ago and I participated in the triathlon, that got me into the biking aspect. The other and most important reason is three of my grandparents have had cancer, one grandmother had breast cancer, the other two had colon cancer. Having them in my life and knowing what they have gone through definitely gets me up the tough hills and helps me face other challenges."

The challenge for these young adults is not just the ride, but to raise money as well. Everyone who participates is expected to raise $4,500 each. Natalie says her fundraising is at the $6,500 level and these young adults can keep raising dollars while they ride, from people they meet and from those who might be inspired to go online and donate to the cause.

You can hear the enthusiasm and purpose in Natalie's voice as she talks about the ride. "A lot of people consider our journey across the country almost like their fight against cancer," she says. "Knowing we are fighting right along with them, (on our ride), gets them going especially on the tougher days." And there are some tough days.

Natalie and friends

On the two different occasions I spoke to Natalie, she was completing rides of 102 miles and then 105 miles in a single day! The riders start early about 5am, have a short window to get their duffel bag and backpack into the van which travels with them, and then for everyone to check their golden treasure...their bike, to make sure it is in proper working order, including brakes and tires, because sometimes things break down.

One of those breakdowns has left an indelible scar on the hearts, minds and souls of all the riders in the 4K for Cancer Cause.

Natalie explains: "On Friday, June 13th, Jamie Roberts was in a tragic accident. She and another girl on Team Portland were hit while changing a tire on the side of the road near Lexington, Kentucky). The other girl was injured and is doing OK, but Jamie was not so fortunate, she did not survive the accident. It has been very difficult for all of the 4K for Cancer teams, but through Jamie's passing, we have a renewed passion for our ride and have grown much closer as a team. We now ride for Jamie and all those she rode for in addition to our own."

It was this turn of events, after my first discussion with Natalie, which led me to postpone the Sunday Series last week, while the riders and their families dealt with the news. All of the riders shut down for 48 hours, in honor of Jamie. Brock Yetso, CEO of the 'The Ulman Cancer Fund' issued this statement: "Jamie's selflessness, her commitment to serving others and her deep devotion to her friends, family and fellow riders was apparent to everyone who knew her. All of us at the Ulman Cancer Fund extend our deepest condolences to Jamie's family, whose grief must be boundless at this time. We, and all of our 4K for Cancer riders, will carry Jamie's memory with us in our hearts as we continue serving the mission that Jamie cared so deeply about."

Natalie says Jamie's death has drawn everyone on the team closer, if that's even possible. She says she was "blown away" how close everyone had become even a few days into the ride. The turn of events in the past week has just made that bond even stronger.

The ride continues, though with a heavy heart for the loss of one of their own. But just like the fight against cancer, to give up now would be like giving in. The goal is to finish the ride and improve the lives of young adults battling every day to fight the disease. The slogan for the Ulman Cancer Fund for Young Adults: Cancer Changes Lives... So Do WE!

And these brave young adults riding across America are making it happen for their peers, who like the riders, are facing uphill challenges everyday. Those dealing with illness have a destination...to be cancer-free. But unlike those riding cross-country in their honor, these cancer victims are not always sure of the path to get where they want to go, it can be scary, uncertain and sometimes result in an untimely end. The riders hope to give these fighters direction, support, hope, encouragement and precious dollars to secure their path to freedom.

If you are so inspired, you can do your part as well. Join Natalie and her team, honor Jamie and her memory and help more than 100 other young riders from Team Seattle, Team San Francisco, Team San Diego and Team Portland, all on a summer tour to help do more: (http://4kforcancer.org/), (http://ulmanfund.org/), (https://www.facebook.com/4kforcancer).

And don't just take my words for it....you can also follow Natalie's words on her own blog: (http://nat-attack14.tumblr.com/)

To all those riders making their way along the 4K – God's speed, ride safe, be strong and thanks for being there.

Until next time, thanks for taking the time.

The Sunday Series: #JennStrong

Z'We've been honored to have our journey chronicled and our leukemia story told by the man we call The Blade. My wife has dodged cancer twice and each time the humanity, kindness and generosity shown by the community has touched us. Having our story told allowed folks to lend support to Jenn. No one fights alone.

—Nestor and Jenn Aparicio

A gift. Sometimes it can come from the most unexpected place, sometimes from a giver you never meet and sometimes, it might save a life.

Just ask Jennifer Aparicio.

On a warm June night, the gift of life slowly dripped into Jenn's own body, to create a new beginning. One-hundred days before that moment, life turned on a dime, but on this night Jenn was cashing in. The chance at not just a new life, but any life. A life saved and the chance to journey onward.

It was mid-March when Jenn felt pain and soreness just under her right armpit, maybe a weird reaction to a spider bite she received while she and her husband Nestor were on vacation in Australia. But upon closer inspection, the couple thought it might be something much more. Sometimes intuition is like a premonition, in this case it was. It was much more. But what it was, no one could be sure. And that was a problem.

"They didn't even say leukemia in the beginning," says Jenn. They just said, "your blood, all your counts are really low, we want you to go to the emergency room right now and we want you to get admitted. We want you to see a hematologist. Go to the emergency room, they will have a hematologist there to look at your blood." Then the doctors had Jenn and Nestor put on surgical masks and told them to pack a bag. Jen says, "I didn't think I was coming home, but they said, grab a few things and plan to spend the night, not knowing it would be *forty-one nights.*"

After an extremely painful bone marrow biopsy, the doctors at Johns Hopkins Hospital in Baltimore diagnosed leukemia. Initial diagnosis day was the afternoon of March 20th, and as fate would have it, just hours before, Nestor was announcing his return to Baltimore radio, his greatest love. Now the love of his life was in trouble. It's crazy how life presents you with the highest of highs and the lowest of lows almost at the same moment – and then asks what are you going to do now? The juxtaposition of life events can bring even the strongest to their knees, but the Aparicio's were not letting this news destroy them. They talked about how they would tell their family and then their friends, co-workers, their large social media following on Facebook, (https://www.facebook.com/nastynestor?fref=ts), and Twitter, (https://twitter.com/NestorAparicio), and Nestor's radio audience, (http://wnst.net/). They decided to go public with almost everything, though they held back a lot. "People think we've shared a lot. We've shared just a teaspoon of what has really happened, literally," says Nestor.

And so much has happened. As soon as the diagnosis was made, intense chemotherapy began, literally the next day. And though the initial hospital stay lasted five weeks, Jenn says it was a blessing to be there. "The good part of being admitted," says Jenn, "is they are on top of your medication to avoid the nausea and the headaches. I never got sick at the hospital." She also never felt sorry for herself. "It's funny, in the beginning I never said, 'why me?' I just didn't think it mattered. All that mattered was how are we going to fix it, how are we going to get through this, what's our next step?"

I sat next to Jenn on a couch in the Aparicio's downtown Baltimore condominium for this interview, as she spoke these words, you could feel they are at the heart of how she and Nestor decided to handle this journey. They are turning adversity into advantage, for themselves and just as importantly for other people. That's how you live a life, to take the obstacle you are up against and use it to make life better for others, in this case, to save lives.

Nestor says, "she got this disease which probably would have killed her 40 years ago, probably would have killed her 30 years ago and maybe would have killed her 20 years ago. You know when they looked at her on March 20th, they weren't saying 'you're among the people that are positively going to beat this.' They were saying, 'we gotta figure this out' and now they're saying, 'she's going to be fine.' The hardest part is beating the cancer and then having a match. That's the daily double. And I'm telling you the one thing we are going to do the rest of our lives is get people registered, (to be swabbed), so that if it's your daughter, your niece, your nephew, your uncle, our neighbor, your friend... that they will have a chance to live."

It is literally finding a donor for the bone marrow transplant, and getting the transplant completed that saved Jenn's life. The donor is anonymous, the Aparicio's believe, actually are pretty certain, the donor came from overseas. But if not for swabbing to register bone marrow donors and find a match, miracles like Jenn's might never happen. That is why there are websites like, (http://bethematch.org/), to educate others and encourage others to get swabbed, get registered and save lives. As the website so eloquently states, "the cure for blood cancers like leukemia is in the hands of ordinary people."

You and I can make a difference. It's why Jenn and Nestor have teamed up with There Goes My Hero, (http://theregoesmyhero.org/), to get the message out to the masses, to hold drives where others are educated and can donate time, money and themselves, by getting registered.

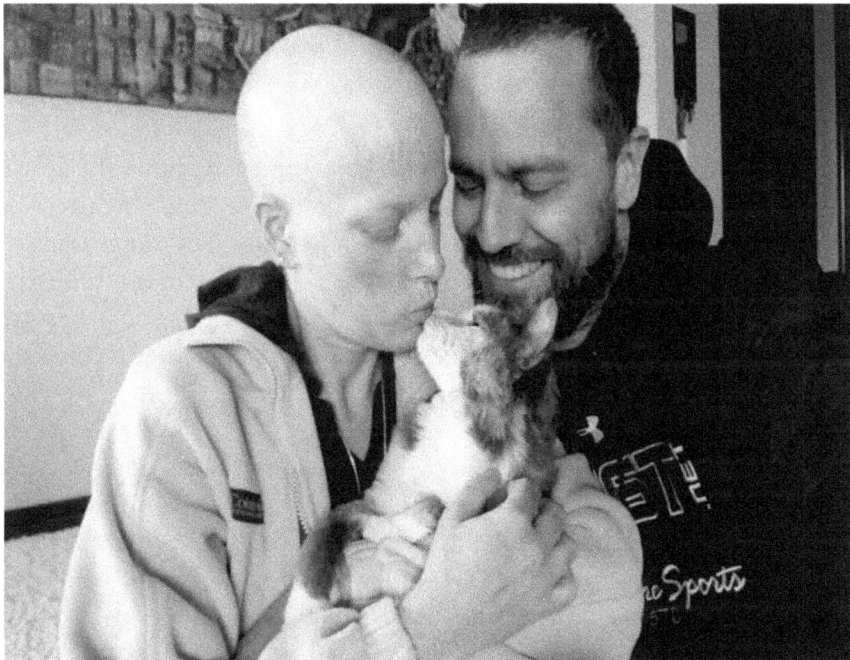

There Goes My Hero founder and leukemia survivor Erik Sauer on the radio with Nestor Aparicio and Marlon Brown of the Baltimore Ravens at Hightopps in Timonium

Fifty-thousand people are diagnosed with leukemia each year in the United States. Jenn has an extremely rare form of leukemia that has characteristics of both lymphoblastic and myelogenous leukemia. But no matter the type, if a stem cell or blood marrow match cannot be found, too many won't make it. Jenn and Nestor witnessed plenty of stories of hopes lost, lives devastated, others losing loved ones, as they spent what seemed like weeks-on-end at the hospital.

Even family members are not always the answer to finding a cure. "Your siblings only have a 25% chance of being a match," says Jenn." My sister, even if she was a match, we probably wouldn't have used her bone marrow, because she was diagnosed with MS a few years ago." Nestor continues, "so the ask for people is to get swabbed and that's something everybody can do or give a donation to causes like There Goes My Hero or come out and support our events. You know this is a lifetime sentence for us. We'll be doing this forever, keeping this scoreboard of how many lives we can save, because I saw what happened last night in that hospital room and it's miraculous, that's all I can say."

There's also the miracle of support. "Everybody said the same thing," says Nestor, "blank check...what can I do to help you, what can I do for you right now?" I said to Jenn, "the thing that's going to save your life is this swabbing, and that's it, that's the reason I was supposed to be back on the air (radio) now. I felt like by coming back on the air I could do a lot more good for causes like this and I want to live in the moment and do the most I can and the best I can. Hence the name of the show, *The Happy Hours*. This is why I call the show *The Happy Hours*, because I want to make people feel good."

Life takes you strange places, the journey has twists and turns you can never anticipate, but when they come, it's all in how you react to them. I asked Jenn about her biggest takeaway from all of his and her answer is on target–"Mindset is everything. Remaining positive is what's gotten us through. I mean I have some down moments, but you know I was diabetic for 23 years and never knew my blood type until I got my transfusion and it was B-Positive. And I put that on my Facebook page and I said, that's not only my blood type, but my mantra. Be positive. I'm thankful for where I am, I'm lucky to be where I am." (https://www.facebook.com/jennesa1?fref=ts).

It's not just Jenn's blood type, but her answer to that question, which proves why the campaign for her is called, #BmorePositive and #JennStrong. There I was sitting on the couch next to a vibrant, articulate, beautiful cancer survivor, who less than a day before had a bag of stem cells dripped into her body to create a new life, to save her life and the life she shares with Nestor.

In turn, Nestor shared similar sentiments about his takeaway from this experience —"There's a Rush line, 'we're only immortal for a limited time,' right? I identify with music, I would say we have not at all lived our lives, you know. We are watching the World Cup right now, but we know what it's like to sit in Germany and watch the United States play Italy, cause we did it. We see people put pictures up of Bora Bora, we know what it's like, cause we've been there. We see people that wish they could go to a Super Bowl, we've been to ten. We've done a lot of things and then first thing I think we did after the night Jenn got sick, I went over to the hospital and I said, 'let's talk about what we're going to do when you get better.' We started putting a bucket list together. Live like you were dying right, do it now, don't wait, right now, like the Van Halen song, *Right Now.*"

Now is the moment. Now it's your turn. Get swabbed, share hope and help save a life. Be the same person Jennifer Aparicio is showing the whole world, #JennStrong.

Until next time, thanks for taking the time.

The Sunday Series: Saving the World

A lot of people were just lying there. Many of them with broken arms and broken legs and telling me I would be sorry. I figured well, I'm here now, I'm stuck.

—Staff Sergeant Harvey Brotman

70-years removed from living it the memories for Harvey Brotman are still pretty vivid.

Exactly one year after the day which "will live in infamy," when the Japanese bombed Pearl Harbor, Harvey Brotman and two friends decided it was time to make a move. "I went down with two buddies to enlist," says Harvey "because we knew we'd be drafted anyway." Two of us got accepted, the other guy didn't make it because of a hearing issue." The initial experience seemed almost routine to Harvey. But what Harvey couldn't know then was he would become part of one of the greatest military invasions in the history of the world.

The first stop for Harvey and his friend was Fort Meade, Maryland and then quickly on to Abilene, Texas. Abilene was tough – sand, desert, and constant wind storms. Harvey, now Private Brotman, says, "they would march us into sandstorms...sand hitting us in the face, your food was covered with sand, you had to keep brushing it off before you could eat. Finally, someone came to me and asked if I would like to go to Fort Benning, Georgia. I figured why not, any place is better than here. Then they told me the news, "there's just one thing you'll have to do though, jump out of a plane in flight. I said I would do it, just to get out of Texas."

When Harvey got off the train at Fort Benning, it wasn't a pretty sight. "A lot of people were just laying there," says Harvey. "Many of them with broken arms and broken legs and telling me I would be sorry. I figured well, I'm here now, I'm stuck. We did a lot of training, a lot of running, exercising and they took us out to show us how to pack the parachute. If you were going to jump, you had to have confidence in the chute you packed." Pack, jump, practice. Harvey was now part of the 101st Airborne Division at Fort Benning, the Screaming Eagles. And before he knew it, Harvey was being called to head overseas. Destination: England.

It wasn't an easy trip by any stretch of the imagination. The paratroopers left from New York on a ship bound for Europe, but the engine went bad and the men had to spend the next 30 days in Newfoundland. Then it was on to Halifax, Nova Scotia to pick up supplies. Except the ship had an accident pulling into port and it took 45 days to get a new one.

Eventually, these paratroopers made it to England. Harvey says he stayed in Hungerford and practiced, practiced, practiced. "We did a lot of training, a lot of jumping," says Harvey. "We did a jump on a very windy day and we lost about 50 percent of the guys with broken arms and broken legs, but I was OK."

As World War II took a turn, the Allied Forces planned for a massive invasion of France, on the beaches of Normandy. Harvey was about to play a part in the climactic battle of the war, D-Day. At 12am on June 6th, 1944, Harvey and his fellow paratroopers boarded one of the more than nine-hundred C47s which flew into France, five hours in advance of the ground invasion of D-Day. "At 12:55am we jumped out of the plane, but I landed in the wrong place, there was no one around. I had a clicker I used for identification and if you got a click-click in return, you knew someone was nearby. I clicked, but got no response, and it was pitch black, so I stayed in a hedgerow until it got light. Then I saw the 82nd airborne, I identified myself and told them I was from the 101st Airborne and they let me stay with them for four days to battle until I was sent back to my unit."

Private Brotman's primary responsibility in battle was as a medic, to aid the wounded. But Harvey couldn't save one of his own. The man who became his best friend in the service was shot and killed on the first day of battle. Harvey says when you're 20-years-old, far from the safety of home and your friend is killed, that's a tough pill to swallow, you can't understand why, or how this is happening. A devastating repercussion of one of the toughest days of World War II.

Harvey's group was part of the 502nd Parachute Infantry Regiment. That group eventually ended up taking Sainte-Mère-Église in France and remained there until it was time to head to Holland. Harvey and the other surviving paratroopers would jump into Arnhem, Holland, a strategic location on the banks of the Rhine River. The Battle of Arnhem, part of Operation Market Garden, was fought in September 1944. It was during this invasion into Holland that Harvey took a piece of shrapnel in his chest, eventually leading to his being awarded the Purple Heart.

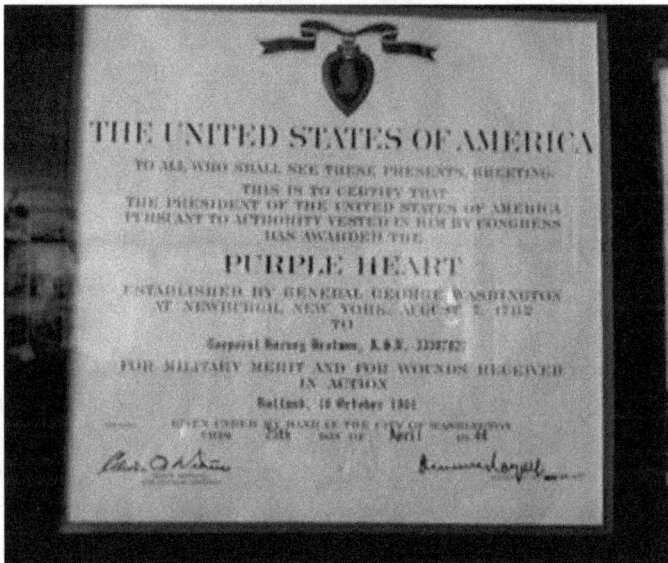

After the eventual success by Allied Forces in Holland, it was onto Bastogne, Belgium, where Harvey and many of the 101st Airborne were in bad shape. It was the worst," says Harvey. "It was so cold, snow, freezing temperatures, very, very bad. I went and got newspaper to shove into everyone's boots to try and stop the onslaught of frostbite. We were surrounded by Germans and there were no planes to come rescue us because it was always cloudy and snowing. The Germans wanted us to surrender." But on Christmas Day, (1944), the clouds finally gave way and the bombers moved in and the besieged American forces were relieved by General George Patton's Third Army. "We didn't think we were going to get out of there," says Harvey, "not until Patton showed up."

Harvey says one of the highlights of the war for him was actually getting to meet General Patton. On the way back from a short leave in England, Harvey was asked to do an inspection, and it turned out it was Patton who was conducting it. Harvey says Patton told him and the others, "go back and tell your Colonel you are a god damn good-looking bunch of men, go back and tell him that." Harvey did just that, relaying the message back from one of the greatest war heroes of all time. Harvey says when not in battle, he and the other paratroopers were a great looking bunch of men. "Our boots shined like crazy and our uniforms were always just right."

Harvey survived WWII and made it through the ranks during those years, going from Private, to Private First Class, to Corporal and then to Staff

Sergeant. Harvey says his greatest takeaway from his experience overseas and in battle: Life.

"Life is most meaningful," says Harvey. Losing his best friend on the first day of the invasion brought that reality home in a hurry. "I learned a lot about life and there were so many nice people I met in France and England."

But it might have been a telegram he sent home which meant the most in Harvey's life and to his mom back home in Baltimore.

Harvey was an only child. His father was killed in a car accident when Harvey was only 10-years-old, so it was just he and his mother living alone until the day he left to join the war. Because Harvey's parachute took him far from the assigned landing spot on D-Day, the military sent a telegram home to his mother, relaying to her that her 20-year-old son was missing in action. It wasn't until Harvey got a 30-day leave and could send another telegram home that his mother knew the real story. He told her he was fine. Ms. Brotman's only child had survived.

A room in Harvey's apartment is now adorned with pictures and awards from his time in the service. A Purple Heart, a Bronze Star, the French Croix De Guerre, the European-African Middle-Eastern Campaign Medal, a Good Conduct Medal, and the WWII Victory Medal. Harvey has saved them all.

And why not? Harvey Brotman helped save the world.

Until next time, thanks for taking the time.

The Sunday Series: Get Your Motor Runnin'

The difference is in how Robert spreads the message and that is without fear, or embarrassment. It would be easy to be uneasy.

–Mark Brodinsky

Get your motor runnin', head out on the highway. Looking for adventure in whatever comes our way.

–Lyrics from Born To Be Wild

Robert Kaitz put it off for way too long, it was barely an issue, besides he's a man. Kaitz was owner of a successful computer business with 500 clients and 5000 computers worldwide. A tough guy, member of a motorcycle club, loved to party and have fun. When you're a man like that, there's not much that can hold you back or take you down. Certainly not a minor ache or pain.

Robert says he had experienced acid reflux for years, but as he kept banging on his chest to stop the indigestion, something was unusual. Just below the left nipple, a tiny bump. Probably just another cyst Robert thought, he had had several removed from his back, not a big deal. But when the bump eventually got painful he reluctantly went to the doctor.

"I'm pissed I didn't go sooner", says Robert. "But I didn't think guys could get it." He's right, in a way, because the odds are only one-in-1,000 for men, not like the 1-in-8 for women. But the odds in life are not always in your favor. For Robert Kaitz, he was suddenly odd man out...he had breast cancer.

The Ribbons are Pink
But should be Pink & Blue
Women get Breast Cancer
But Men Get It Too!

Copyright 2005 John W. Nick Foundation

Surgery was scheduled immediately to remove the cancerous tumor, which by now was Stage-3. A radical mastectomy, 25 lymph nodes removed, five of them positive for cancer. Chemotherapy and radiation next, and a new lease on life. Robert was ready to share his story, but it wasn't easy, still isn't.

He says, "people look at you funny when you say you have male breast cancer. People smile like you are kidding when you tell them you have breast cancer. But hopefully, we are making a difference."

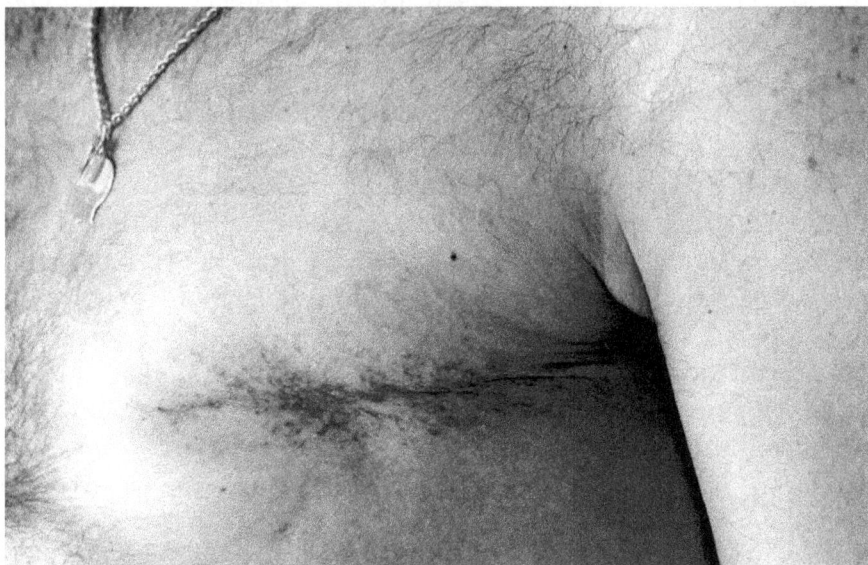

The difference is in how Robert spreads the message and that is without fear or embarrassment. And it would be easy to be uneasy. As part of the treatment for the breast cancer, he was given tamoxifen, the same drug prescribed to women who experience the same disease. Robert was dealing with the same side effects women do, sweating, hot flashes, and mood swings. "When I first got diagnosed and received treatment and then tried to get out here and tell people, many were surprised," says Robert. "I got up in front of a bunch of bikers, men and told them about the breast cancer and the side effects of the medication I was on. No one could believe it. But if I can help one guy not be a stubborn ass**** like me, then I have done a good job."

And Robert's cancer journey was not over just yet. In 2009, he was diagnosed with prostate cancer. Because he had genetic testing after the breast cancer, the prostate cancer was caught early and his prostate removed. Robert says if he hadn't had the testing, it might not have been picked up. The double whammy only served to make him more determined to share his story.

In December 2009, Robert sold his computer business and now travels the country, on his motorcycle or in his big RV, raising awareness, especially about the male breast cancer and early detection of any disease. His journey has received national attention. He was invited to visit the 'The Dr. Oz Show,' in a program which aired in January 2010 and helped to shine the spotlight on diseases which typically are associated with women, but can also affect men. Robert says there was a woman in the audience who said she came to the show, but her husband refused to come. Robert told the female audience member, "when you are intimate with him, feel his breast and if you feel a lump grab him like a fish on a hook and drag him to the doctor!"

And this is where part of the problem lies, says Robert: "The biggest issue with male breast cancer is men are dying from it. Only one percent of all breast cancer cases are men, but twenty-five percent of those men die from the disease because they catch it so late, they are simply not aware."

And too late is no good for Robert. His experience with cancer has taught him a couple of things, besides his desire to share and educate others. Robert is a member of the Legion Motorcycle Club, (http://www.legionmc.com/). Everyone in the club has a nickname, his is Atlas, for a good reason. "Because I carry the weight of the world on my shoulders. I will give the shirt off my back for anyone to help them. If you get out of bed and you hate the day ahead, come talk to me." And Robert doesn't just talk the talk, he walks the walk. If there's one thing he says he's learned, it's to live life and enjoy, because life is short.

Robert says, "don't put something off that you will do another day, that you want to do, because you will probably never do it. Don't sweat the small stuff, if you don't worry too much it works out. Work it out and move forward."

A big part of that forward progress is Robert's participation in the John W. Nick Foundation, (https://www.malebreastcancer.org/), an organization dedicated to male breast cancer and to the man, John W. Nick, who died from the disease at age 58. Awareness could have saved his life and Robert is on a mission to save the lives of other men. "Do normal checkups and get physicals and stay on top of everything," he says. "The key is catching this stuff early, if you don't catch it early, then there is trouble. If you find it now you can fix it, if you find it later, it might be too late."

Just like the lyrics from, Born to be Wild, Robert is gonna make it happen, take the world in a love embrace. If he can save even one life, or make that life better, then the ride is worth it.

Until next time, thanks for taking the time.

The Sunday Series: Life in "Perspektive"

Mark has an ability to bring emotion and love to words like few do. There are thousands of decisions we make each day and these decisions will either deplete us or replenish us. Reading Mark's work fills the tank every single time. He's a star. The world needs more Mark Brodinsky! #partofthebillion

–Pete Kohlasch

An uphill battle. His team down by nine points heading into the 3rd quarter of the state championship game and the biggest game of this young man's life. This quarterback, the leader of his Harrison High School football team, suddenly takes off for a 50-yard touchdown run, cutting the deficit to only two points.

Two to tie, three to win. 4th quarter. Two seconds to go. One last chance.

It's not a run, it's not a pass. This quarterback kicks a field goal to win the state championship by a single point. A victory by the slimmest of margins with nearly no time remaining. For Pete Kohlasch, this was a huge moment, more dramatic than he had ever experienced, on the biggest stage of his life. For Pete, this was a turning point. In that moment, a leader was born.

There is no doubt victory and the incredible success in leading his high school team to the state championship was a defining moment for Pete

Kohlasch, but being made to feel small was also as big a motivator in his leadership development. "One of my first jobs out of college, I was in a sales meeting and I am sitting at a round table of sorts and I communicate this great idea," says Pete. "A colleague of mine turns to me and says, 'you are not paid to be a visionary, you are paid to sell.' I don't think I was in that role for another month. I will be damned to be told I'm not a visionary or paid to be one. It's a moment I will never forget."

Being made to feel small has energized Pete to act big. And his actions, his heart, his smarts are all about you. Life for Pete is all about...you. He thinks about you, he plans for you, he wants to give back to you, he wants you to enjoy the life you were meant to live.

It comes from deep within Pete's heart and it actually began long ago. "When I was a kid in an assembly in 3rd grade and saw a speaker on stage, or watching a TV program, or hearing a motivational speaker – I just knew from an early age, I wanted to make an impact on other people. My mother and my grandmother did a great job of feeding me quotes and inspirational stories. I used to write poetry a little bit, I enjoy writing. Growing up, I always had a notebook filled with thoughts and ideas."

Pete means what he says. He is an idea man. Many say it, but actions speak louder than words. At only 29 years of age, Pete wrote and developed a live and virtual coaching program called Path to Mindfulness. Pete has helped to direct and transform the lives of people from all walks of life, from a 62-year-old chiropractor to a 23-year-old financial services professional. Just a few months ago, Pete headed west and spent a week in San Jose, California to learn from the best, Brendon Burchard, author of *The Millionaire Messenger, The Golden Ticket, The Charge*, and a man who runs a High Performance Academy. Pete came home certified as a High Performance Coach.

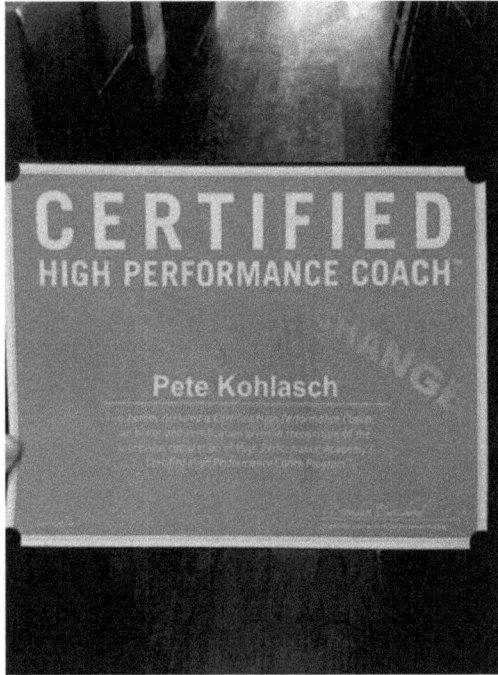

Pete says there has been a turning point recently. "When I'm reading or getting certified or listening to someone speak, in my mind I'm thinking how can I translate this to the people I work with, it went from self-serving to how can I use this to help other people. It's been a transformation in my coaching."

The core of Pete's business is something called PerspeKtive. That's not a misspelling, it's spelled that way for a reason, including the first and last initials in Pete's name. His mission is clear: to positively impact the lives of other people through coaching and civic collaboration. Pete's business is built on this platform: "Individuals shape society, but collaboration moves the world." He also believes, as do I, in the message of business philosopher Jim Rohn: "Work harder on yourself than you do on your job. If you work hard at your job, you make a living, work hard on yourself, you make a fortune." Pete says since the moment he heard those words, he has seen the benefit of working hard on himself and he is excited to help others and change lives.

Besides building his coaching platform, Pete is working hard with other civic leaders on projects designed to invoke positive change in the community. He's been selected as a member of the Give Class, (http://www.businessvolunteersmd.org/volunteer/give-program/current-give-class/), and as a Rising Star, a program presented as part of the Living Classrooms by the Baltimore Business Journal. This is a select group of young professionals recognized for their professional achievements and philanthropic efforts.

All of this takes great effort, helping to exact change in the world is no easy business. Building your own personal growth business and being a true leader in your community takes dedication, discipline, and devotion and is not without struggle. You have to want it so badly and at the same time help convince others they too can build bigger lives. But the payoff is worth it. For Pete, this is what he wants to do with his life. Remember, he is always thinking about **you**.

It's Pete's gift. "I have a genuine desire to help others," Pete says. "To be free to create and serve. Always helping others to positively transform their lives so I can be remembered as someone who cared immensely, loved intensely and lived with great passion, purpose and intention." And Pete's not blowing smoke, watching him say those words in our interview, I can see in his eyes how much this all means to him. It comes from deep within.

Pete's parents were divorced when he was only 2-years-old. His stepfather came into his life a few years later and the two developed a very close relationship. Pete says instead of being resentful about the divorce, he feels very fortunate because he feels like he has done a good job of taking the best from all three of his parents: "Take the best and leave the rest," Pete says. "I think everybody teaches us something."

With the nephews

There is no doubt he's on the right track. Just read these words from Pete's mentor, Brendon Burchard from his book, The Charge: "The world really has changed to favor a new kind of worker, what I call the creative collaborator. The person who can be individually creative at work yet socially adept and tuned in when collaborating with others is the one who wins."

Remember Pete's own vision for Perspektive: "Individuals shape society, but collaboration moves the world." It's Pete's personal mission, the one he created on his own. A true visionary.

Every person Pete helps in transforming their own life moves the world another inch in the right direction. Add up those inches and soon we have feet, yards, miles and more. If more people reach for their dreams, the entire world benefits. (http://yourperspektive.com/)

Attract Greater Success & Happiness In Life & Work

With all transparency, I can tell you Pete has taught me much. I am fortunate to be part of a mastermind group with Pete and two other men I hold in the highest regard; realtor and motivator, Rob Commodari and financial advisor and giver, Mark Pallack. These men are not just mentors and friends, they are now my brothers. I urge anyone who has the desire to form their own group to do so *today* and watch it change your life, the way these three men have changed mine. Pete feels the same way I do: "When I started in this group I was 26-years-old and I get the opportunity to engage with three older men for whom I have tremendous respect. The accountability and consistency in my life come from that group. What contributes most to your success is who you surround yourself with and connect with and the mastermind group has been the largest contributor to my personal and professional growth."

I can tell Pete it goes both ways. I am living it, I see it in action, as he touches not just my life, but so many others. I have been on this earth two decades longer than Pete Kohlasch, old enough to be his older brother, heck, in an imperfect world, old enough to be his father. And I can share with you from deep within me that this young man is the most genuine, dedicated, hard-working, focused, energetic soul, I have had the pleasure to meet along my way in life. His passion and purpose for what he is trying to do for other people is heartfelt and real. He is truly a rising star, but a star shines most bright when surrounded by others. Pete's mission is to be that star, but to bring others with him, to help **you** create the life **you** deserve.

"Begin with the end in mind," says Pete. "Have clarity about what you want and what you are striving for. Once you have a sense of clarity, it is easier to create a game plan to get there. Once you have the game plan, then you have a new sense of energy and enthusiasm." Nobody does this better than the high school quarterback who led his team to a dramatic victory in the state championship. A leader was born that day and because of that moment, we all get to win.

Until next time, thanks for taking the time.

The Sunday Series: Amanda's Sunrise

I've learned to stay positive and definitely have a greater appreciation for life. Going through all of this has made my family stronger. I never saw my parents upset, they always stayed strong for me and motivated me to keep going. My sisters are my best friends and Madison is my hero. How close we are... I don't even know how to describe it.

–Amanda Endres

Just days away from a major milestone in her life, 17-year-old Amanda Endres is feeling good. She's a fighter. She's determined and she is looking forward to a ton of tomorrows. But the future wasn't always so bright.

Almost 10 years have passed and though only eight-years-old at the time, Amanda still remembers. She was feeling really tired, cold all the time, her stomach hurt, she had fevers, the doctors kept telling her parents it was just the flu. But after a blood test, the doctors changed their story. Amanda had pneumonia... that part would have been easy to take, if there also wasn't another diagnosis, a blood cancer called, Acute Lymphoblastic Leukemia, (ALL), (http://www.cancer.org/cancer/leukemia-acutelymphocyticallinadults/detailedguide/leukemia-acute-lymphocytic-what-is-all).

Next up a three-week hospital stay and Amanda feeling scared and sad. Her sisters, Jacquelyn, Madison and Sydney weren't allowed to visit because of the fear of infection. Amanda was missing a ton of school and then there was the chemotherapy. Rounds of chemo, until the doctors felt she was in remission from the disease, at least enough to go home, yet it was just the beginning.

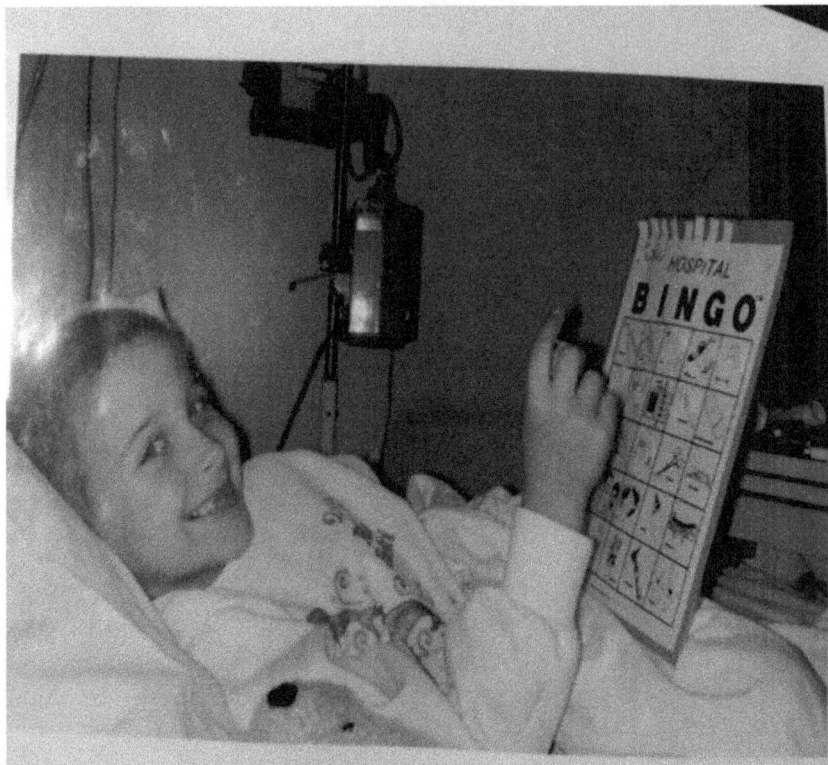

The outpatient treatment lasted 2-1/2 years, chemotherapy to continue to wage the battle and to stop the disease from staging a comeback. It seemed to be working, until one day on the soccer field when Amanda started feeling dizzy and had to leave the game. The cancer had returned. Another hospital stay, just as long as the first just three years before, and the chemo continued. "The chemotherapy was stronger this time," says Amanda, "because I was more high risk, but at least I had expectations of what was going to happen. I missed out on more school and that really upset me because I was determined to have perfect attendance at school that year."

Round two seemed to do the trick, but Amanda was forced to keep up the routine of outpatient chemotherapy treatments, facing the consequences that come with it, fatigue, feeling sick and hair loss. She says her parents and her sisters were and still are her greatest supporters, helping her to battle through it all. But there's also the ray of light which comes from Camp Sunrise.

Established by the American Cancer Society back in 1987, the camp started with only seven campers. Today the week-long camp, maintained and sponsored by Johns Hopkins Sidney Kimmel Comprehensive Cancer Center's Division of Pediatric Oncology, serves over 100 campers. And one of those 100, Amanda Endres, says it changed her life: "All the people at Camp Sunrise inspired me to keep going. All the stories from kids like me and the terrific counselors. They are like my second family. When I'm there, I have no worries about being different. All the people understand me in a way no one else can." This year marked Amanda's 9th year visiting the camp.

But while Camp Sunrise kept her spirits up, some bad cells continued to keep her down. Another relapse in November of 2013 and another round of chemotherapy. But with the pounding her body was taking from the poison, the doctors said they needed another direction for treatment, a bone marrow transplant. Fortunately for Amanda, her 11-year-old sister, Madison was a "half-match" and Johns Hopkins had developed a procedure called a haploidentical transplantation, which had been successful in curing patients of some cancers and blood cancers. Amanda says her sister Madison, scared of hospitals and needles, was a brave soul and the transplant was a success.

The procedure took place in February of this year, and this Tuesday is a big milestone. August 19th is 180 days since the transplant, a watershed day to measure the success of the procedure. Amanda spent the first 100 days after her transplant at Believe in Tomorrow, the home away from home for some of the children who are treated at Johns Hopkins Oncology center. But now Amanda is back home and will be getting back to school and trying to graduate on time. "It was tough this past year," (her junior year of high school), says Amanda, because of the time in the hospital but she is making strides. She attends The Academy of Health Sciences at PGCC (Prince George's Community College). A new program in Maryland, there Amanda can take her high school classes and some college credits to earn an Associates Degree and her high school diploma all at the same time.

Amanda loves the school and health sciences and as happens so often, her life experiences have given her a direction in life. Amanda wants to be a nurse, specifically a pediatric nurse because as she says, "I look up to them and I want to be a nurse to help kids that are just like me." A mission and a vision to help others because at 17 years of age, Amanda knows what it's like to struggle with a childhood disease, but she wants to give back and she's ready.

While modern science may have saved her life, it's the people in her life that have served as Amanda's best medicine. "I've learned to stay positive and definitely have a greater appreciation for life. Going through all of this has made my family stronger. I never saw my parents upset, they always stayed strong for me and motivated me to keep going. My sisters are my best friends and Madison is my hero. How close we are...I don't even know how to describe it."

Sometimes words are not necessary. Amanda need only look to her family, friends and the incredible experience of Camp Sunrise. For Amanda, all of them light her way toward a better tomorrow.

Until next time, thanks for taking the time.

The Sunday Series: Amazing Grace

It was great to see Mark's story on my sister Vickie in his Sunday Series. Vickie fought a heroic fight against Leukemia until her passing almost three years ago, and Mark's tribute to her, and the grace she displayed, was very moving. It was wonderful for me and my family to see how much Vickie touched others, as evidenced by Mark's beautiful words.

–Hillary Gelfman

"A heart is not judged by how much you love, but by how much you are loved by others."

–The Wizard of Oz to the Tin Man

So simple, so profound, so true. I know for me and I bet for most of you, that one line takes you back to a place from long ago, since many of us came to know that classic film in the early stages of our childhood. A time when innocence and hope are in abundance – a book of life being written, page-by-page, day-by-day, with seemingly no end in sight.

We are all children forever, in the minds, in the eyes and in the hearts of our parents. And the place that heart should never have to go is the place where life is completely turned upside down, a place so dark, an abyss so deep that if there was ever a moment time should stand still, if simply to pay respect to life's greatest tragedy, then this is the moment...the loss of a child.

On August 15th, 31-year-old Victoria "Vickie" Gelfman, passed away from acute myeloid leukemia, exactly 18 months to the day of her diagnosis. On August 19th, she was laid to rest and the words which Oz spoke to the Tin Man about heart and love were on full display, as hundreds filled the giant room, one which was void of enough chairs to hold the many who came to pay their respects...proof of how much this single heart was loved by others.

I never met Vickie, but there I was sitting directly across from her father, observing a grief which is unimaginable. I am the father of two daughters and I cannot fathom the depths of what Dick Gelfman, nor his wife Lenore, are experiencing. And I'm not writing this blog to try and understand, for there is no explanation and I honestly, in the deepest recesses of my heart, the place reserved for life's unconditional love for my own two girls... can't go there.

I worked with Dick Gelfman when I was employed at WJZ-TV in Baltimore. I got to know Dick – a warm, smart, funny man – but I never experienced the pleasure of meeting his three girls, Vickie, Joanna and Hillary. It's my loss – because every life we meet makes an impact on our own – and listening to the story of Vickie's life – so eloquently told by her sisters, Hillary and Joanna – I learned a lot about a life which many of us would serve to emulate.

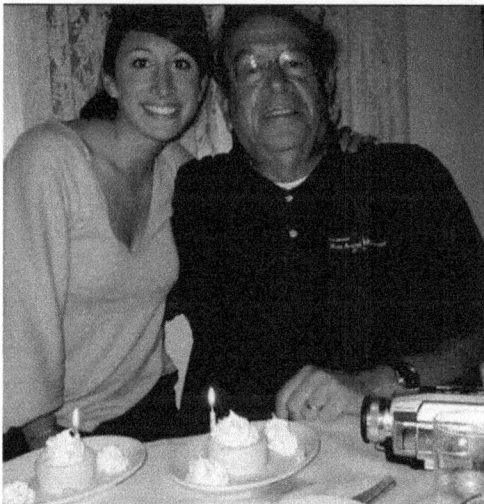

Vickie was a prosecutor in the Howard County State's Attorney's office, a rising star in her field and was known for her ability to develop close relationships with judges, defense attorneys and other prosecutors. She also worked for the House Of Ruth, where she represented victims of domestic abuse. And Vickie was one of the founders of the Ride Across Maryland, an annual motorcycle event that has raised more than $2.5 million for the fight against breast cancer.

A good deal of Vickie's biography is well-told in the pages of the Baltimore Sun: http://www.baltimoresun.com/news/obituaries/bs-md-ob-victoria-gelfman-20140818,0,4653164.story and I encourage you to read it, but it's not the focus of this Sunday Series. I felt compelled to simply share a few observations – because when you witness true love and devotion and understand what legacy is really all about – it is heartwarming. And this is the way, from what I heard and read about Vickie Gelfman, this is the way in which she will be remembered... as an inspiration.

The courage, resolve and in short the ability of Hillary and Joanna to get up and speak, just days after losing their beloved sister and best friend, was in itself inspiring. They shared stories about Vickie's tremendous sense of humor, her determination to become the best in her field, her kind spirit – always the first to help someone else in need – her love of running, her dedication in helping to raise money for causes like breast cancer and serving to fight for victims of domestic abuse, her devotion to her family and her ability to form bonds with others which managed to last a lifetime. So many are part of what is referred to as Team Vickie, as they helped support Vickie in her fight against leukemia and to encourage others in an effort to add donors to the national bone marrow registry, so often the only way to give other leukemia patients a chance at life. Vickie also started her own blog, *The Most Challenging Marathon Yet*, chronicling her battle against the disease – most recently updated by her sister Hillary:

http://vickieuva.wordpress.com/

At Vickie's service there was a pamphlet which included some quotes from family and friends who were fortunate enough to be part of her world:

"Through the efforts of your sisters and your family, the legacy that you all have left through this process certainly makes the world a better place."

"Thank you for teaching us so much about strength and life and grace and dignity."

"You are truly an inspiration. Even during the toughest of times, you manage to be brave, thoughtful and caring."

"You certainly have had an incredible journey, one that no one else I know could have traveled with such class, bravery and determination. It's a journey that has inspired many others by the example you have set and it always will."

And then there was this line from the Broadway show, Wicked:

"It well may be that we will never meet again in this lifetime. So, let me say before we part: So much of me is made of what I learned from you. You'll be with me like a hand-print on my heart. And now whatever way our stories end, I know you'll have rewritten mine by being my friend."

As it turns out one of Vickie's best friends in life is Carly Hughes, one of the lead singers in the Broadway show, Beautiful: The Carole King Story. Just days before Vickie took her final breath, the cast made a YouTube video, with Carly holding up a sign, "We Love You, Vickie." In a moment you will find a link to that incredible song, but first, on this Sunday, I also encourage you to take a moment to think about those you love, especially your children. Maybe it's worth an extra hug, an extra kiss, an extra "I love you" today, for few of us know when the ticks of the clock will stop for us or for them. But if we do it right, and live our life to give to others like Vickie did, *the legacy of love will never end.*

It was Vickie's sister Hillary, who offered the line from the Wizard of Oz, which I posted at the top of this blog. I thank Hillary for taking me back to the moment in my own childhood to remember, but more importantly for simply having the insight to share it – for it is a legacy, because the heart is judged by how much you are loved by others. However, you don't get there unless you love first, then you are touched by life's greatest gift, the opportunity to receive so much more love in return. Life's about love.

In just over three decades on this earth, Vickie Gelfman gave that love, and it is now reflected in how she is remembered... an extraordinary life, one lived simply, in Amazing Grace:

https://www.youtube.com/watch?v=QbiBmgiMSi0

Until next time, thanks for taking the time.

The Sunday Series: Speechless

…but as I gripped my desk with both hands, curled my toes inside my shoes and tilted back my chair in a vain effort to force the words out, I couldn't say them. They were stuck somewhere. Somewhere in between my brain and my heart-breaking effort to turn them into speech.

–Mark Brodinsky

Tomorrow is my 49th birthday. So in honor of the beginning of my 50th year, (after all our birthdays essentially mark the anniversary of the year we just lived, year 50 begins tomorrow), I wanted to share something which I hope will help others. It's the gift I want to give in honor of my own birthday.

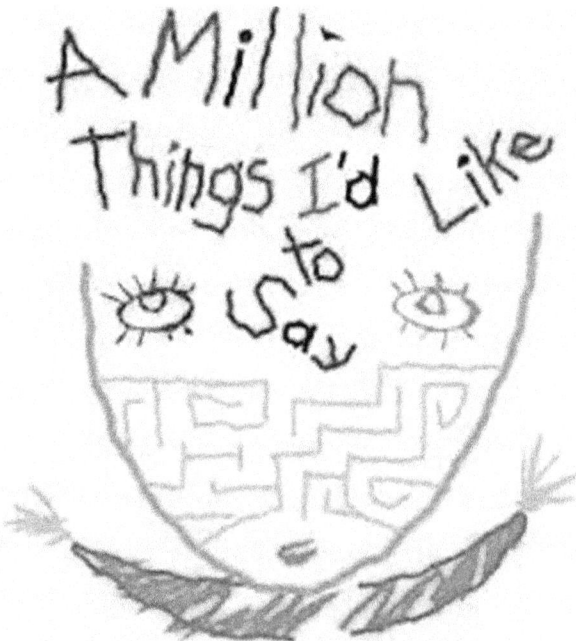

The 4th grade— I still remember it like it was yesterday and I can still see the vision playing out in my mind. Mrs. Cherry, my 4th grade teacher posed a question to the class — and as luck would have it, she called on me. I knew the answer, it was the Declaration of Independence. But as I gripped my desk with both hands, curled my toes inside my shoes and tilted back my chair in a vain effort to force the words out, I couldn't say them. They were stuck somewhere. Somewhere in between my brain and my heart-breaking effort to turn them into speech. The letter "D" was what really had me stuck, because I knew if I uttered that one letter out loud, I would repeat it over-and-over-and-over-and-over before I could complete the answer. I just knew it would come out D-D-D-D-D-Declaration. I didn't know why, but I would stutter and at 10-years-old, that was too much for me to bear. So I pretended I didn't know the answer.

For me that memory was the beginning of the end of a lot of answers I knew, but never said, a lot of information I wanted to share, but was embarrassed and ashamed to do so, a lot of activities I didn't participate in, a lot of people I never interacted with, girls I never asked out and some other choices I made in my life, some of which I might have done differently... and all of because of one reason.

I stutter.

Before I go any further, I want anyone to know, whether young or old, from the bottom of my heart I want you to know, there is nothing wrong with you. It's OK, it really is and if it isn't now, then I want you to do everything in your power to make it OK for you. You are no different. No two people are alike and everyone has things about them which challenge them, which they fight to overcome. Stuttering is simply something you do. Don't let it define who you are.

It wasn't until Rich Polt posted ten questions recently in an article in which he profiled me on his TalkingGood website,

(http://www.talkinggood.com/profiles/MarkBrodinsky), that I even went public with any of this information. I had to because I wanted to be honest and to show others you can overcome. The question was: Tell us something you rarely share in public? So I did. After the story hit Huffington Post, I was immediately contacted by Noah Cornman from

(http://www.say.org/): the Stuttering Association for the Young. We spoke for a while and he asked me to write a blog for them. I decided to take it one step further and share that blog with everyone.

Nothing's gonna hurt you the way that words do

When they settle 'neath your skin

Kept on the inside and no sunlight

Sometimes a shadow wins

For a long, long time I lived underneath the shadow of a speech impediment. As many times as I wanted to, I failed to share with my parents that I had trouble with my speech and I became so adept at avoidance techniques, including NOT saying the things I really wanted to say, that I don't think anyone really knew. But I did and at times it was heartbreaking. My word power increased because I tried to think of any synonym I could to use in place of the words I couldn't seem to utter without a stutter. Words that started with a "d" or an " s" or a " th" or an "m" or an "r" and probably more than I can remember which gave me trouble. I was ashamed, I was scared, and I felt helpless. I've since learned there is nothing to be ashamed of.

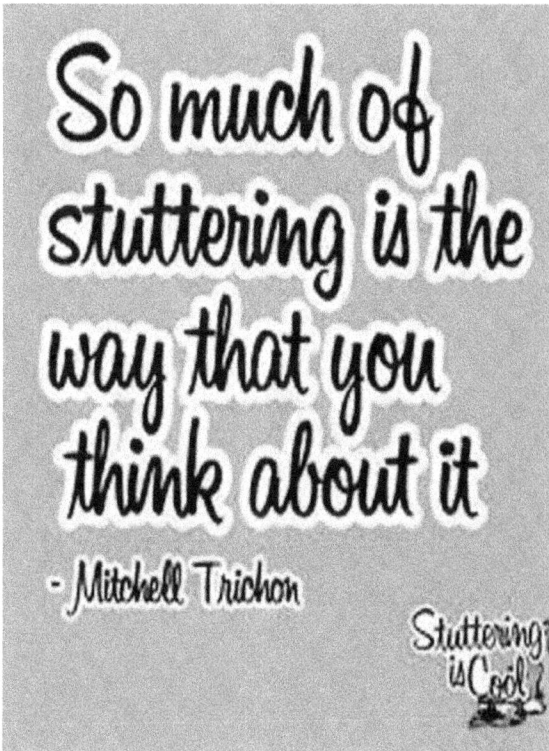

So much of stuttering is the way that you think about it

- Mitchell Trichon

Stuttering is Cool?

The 12th grade. My English teacher, whose name escapes me right now, would do a vocabulary quiz each week where he would say a definition and you would have to give him the word. He would call out names in the class at random to give him the word for the definition and at least two times he called on me... and I actually pretended I didn't know. But I did. The problem was, I was a very good student, on my way to straight "A"'s in multiple semesters my senior year, and this was killing me. I actually scheduled time with him after class, told him about my stuttering, one of the few people I had told up to that point, and asked him NOT to call on me, because of my situation. I told him what letters I had trouble with, we made some type of agreement and I thought it would all be OK. The next week, the first definition he gave he forgot and called on me first— it was one of those words with which I had trouble, but I paused, for what seemed like an eternity and somehow I got through it.

Then there was the high school senior play — I always wanted to act — loved to be "up front and center." The senior class was going to perform Grease, one of my favorite shows. I wanted to give it a shot, wanted my shot, and so I went to the audition. The room was full and I watched as each person who auditioned had to sing a little bit –then read from the script – sight unseen. "I'm going to do this, I can do this," I told myself. But as it got closer to my turn, I started to panic. "What if I can't read what's in front of me," I thought. I couldn't fake it and change the words because others had the same script in their hands and they would all know I couldn't say the words. With only two people to go before my turn, I quietly slipped out. I thought maybe I would just help with the sets or the lights, I never did any of those things. I never participated in the show at all.

I still remember and it still hurts.

Everybody's been there,

Everybody's been stared down by the enemy

Fallen for the fear

And done some disappearing,

Bow down to the mighty

Don't run, just stop holding your tongue

In college, I majored in Mass Communication, with a concentration in Journalism. I was a talented writer, and why wouldn't I be, I possessed a tremendous vocabulary since I had a synonym for nearly every word in the English language.

I needed to have the expansive vocabulary just so I could quickly think of a word to replace the one on which I feared I might stutter. There's still a part of me which thinks I excelled at writing what it was I was afraid to say out loud.

But I also got lucky – because in my senior year at Towson State University – I got an internship at a local TV station, WJZ. That one decision changed my life. From the moment I walked into the newsroom I knew it was where I wanted to be, I had visions of grandeur and thought someday I'm going to be on TV, stutter be damned. I became a writer first, in fact, they hired me part-time while I was still an intern and in school — because I could write, boy, could I write. Then I became the Producer of the WJZ morning show, but I still had this dream of being in front of the camera, not just behind it and most people there knew it.

Eventually, when the news show expanded from an hour to 90 minutes, I got a shot at a segment where from the producer's seat in the control room. I would do an on-camera "tease" for what was coming up later in the show and banter back and forth with the anchors...on the fly, mostly unscripted. I wanted it so bad, I found a way around my stutter, though it wasn't easy. I sometimes spoke too fast, or paused a long time before it was safe to say what I wanted. But when you want it bad enough, when your WHY is that strong, you find a way.

But I wonder what would happen if you

Say what you wanna say

And let the words fall out

That on-air segment gave me confidence to move forward. It wasn't long after that I started dating this girl. This girl's name was Debbie. A name that began with a "D," it was like a nightmare come true. Here I was with this girl I really wanted to be with and there were times I felt I couldn't say her name, especially when others asked me about her and I had to use her name in a sentence. But I was falling in love – and when your WHY is big enough, you find a way. I wasn't going to walk away from this relationship just because I got scared to say her name! I had made too many other detours in my life when it came to speech that I wasn't happy about. I finally broke down, truly broke down and told Debbie my whole story. Then I went for help. Speech therapy, which didn't last long, because my therapist rarely heard me stutter. I was good at this "game" I invented for myself to avoid stuttering, but I did learn some exercises and techniques to confront it. While the sessions did not continue for long, I did gain confidence and still use many of those techniques today.

Maybe there's a way out of the cage where you live

Maybe one of these days you can let the light in

Show me how big your brave is

When I decided to leave the TV business, I became self-employed, offering health insurance and supplemental policies to the self-employed. Guess what the number one word is you must repeat over and over when you talk about health insurance? *Deductible.* The dreaded "d" word. Without being able to say that word, I figured no one would ever buy from me. It was critical. It was mandatory. I practiced it. I took my time, I focused on elongating the vowels and before you knew it, I had sold more than $6 million in policies in a 10-year-span. My family was depending on me to be successful, they needed me and failure was not an option. My WHY, my reason for doing it was bigger than my "challenge."

Say what you wanna say

And let the words fall out

Honestly, I wanna see you be brave

With what you want to say

And let the words fall out

Honestly, I wanna see you be brave

There are plenty more examples of how I let stuttering affect my life in ways it never should, because I am bigger than that challenge and it took me a while to understand how to get there and to stand tall. I want to tell anyone, children or adults, don't let this define who you are, or who you are trying to become. I have much to be proud of. I am an Emmy-Award winner for my ability to *communicate* my ideas, vision, and instructions as producer of a TV news broadcast. I am an Author. I wrote a #1 Amazon Best-Seller and staged a month-long book tour talking to people all the time. I started this blog and *I conduct live phone interviews* for these stories and I am now booking *speaking engagements* to share my story and to help others to lead bigger lives, to find their WHY and to change the world. I am a successful financial services professional – *I talk all day long* to prospects, clients and co-workers. Ask anyone of them and they would be shocked to know that I stutter. But I do.

And I am not ashamed.

And since your history of silence

Won't do you any good,

Did you think it would?

Let your words be anything but empty

Why don't you tell them the truth?

I am telling you the truth. I am telling you because I care. And to the children of SAY, or to any child that stutters – keep your head up, keep learning, keep fighting, keep trying and be proud. I have been where you are and I love you. Don't avoid. Confront. Face it head on and overcome. You can. Say what's in your heart, say what's on your mind. Every voice matters. Find yours and if you need me, reach out. I'm here. I want to see you be BRAVE.

Say what you wanna say

And let the words fall out

Honestly, I wanna see you be brave

Until next time, thanks for taking the time.

The Sunday Series: Larry's Ride

While there are no words to truly express how I feel on the anniversary of my husband's tragic collision, I look back to Mark's post. Mark's words are incredibly meaningful and much appreciated. In his words, Mark captured the heart and soul of who Larry was and what he meant to our family, friends and community. Mark has an amazing ability to present a story of tragedy and sadness, yet leave you feeling hopeful and optimistic once you reach the end. Thank you, Mark, for this post. I read it all the time!—Tami Bensky

It was quite the ride. A ride which would leave an impression on so many that when it ended so abruptly, the loss was devastating, the void so deep it created a virtual chasm in the lives of an entire community.

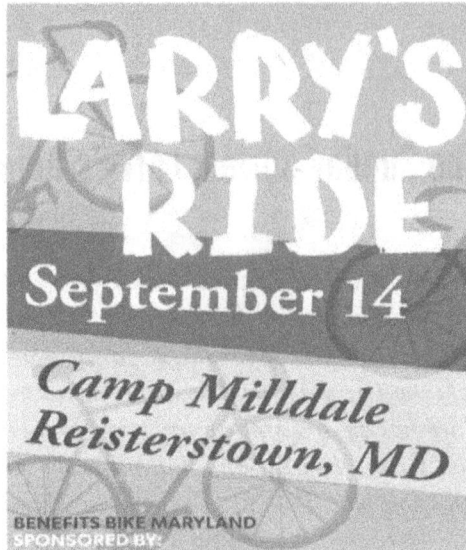

This is not the first time I've shared Larry Bensky's story, but an event taking place today makes it a perfect topic for the Sunday Series. Larry was a friend I met later in life and to be honest, I'm going to share some of the same sentiments I wrote about more than a year ago in this blog, but this time, it's much more about how you make a comeback, how Tami and the girls are moving forward, how today, Sunday, September 14th... Larry's Ride continues. A journey into infinity and beyond.

Larry Bensky's life ended on the back roads of Baltimore County on April 6th, 2010. Larry, an avid cyclist, loved to take afternoon and weekend rides and was always cautious and prepared. But when a driver coming up behind him on that fateful day in April was unprepared to give way, the lives of a close-knit family and the hearts of a community were dragged down into the same dark abyss.

That day a wife lost her husband, two little girls lost their Dad, parents lost a son, an entire community lost a man of integrity, faith and fortitude. Larry made his way through life with determination, drive and tremendous intelligence. He was a good soul, who always did what was right. He loved his family, provided for them and supported them emotionally, financially and unconditionally. He was smart, savvy, and completely unselfish. He loved to talk, to ask questions, to constantly search for answers and to smile. It's what I remember best about him...that smile.

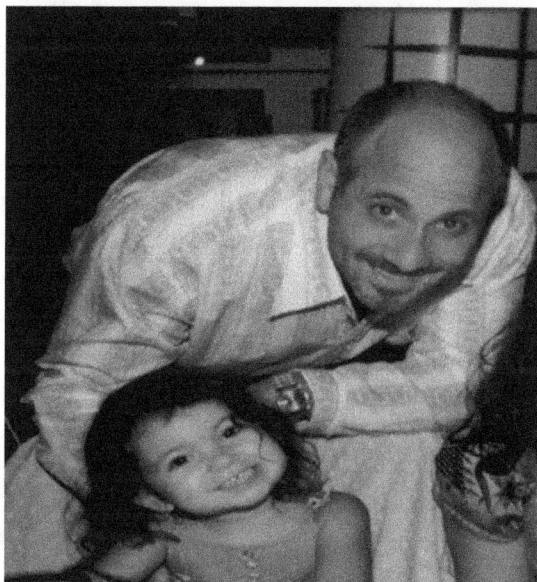

For a long time after his death, smiles were hard to come by. Larry's family and friends were stunned. His wife Tami, his daughters Gabi and Katelyn were to put it mildly, in shock. Larry was the love of Tami's life — it seemed as if life could not go on without him. The feelings of loss were immeasurable, the emptiness seemed too big to overcome, the journey back from the abyss would be a long one.

Larry touched my life and in death touched me again. The day he died was a Tuesday. Just three days later the Bensky family was supposed to come over to our house for dinner with some other friends. I can still remember sitting with my family at dinner that fateful Tuesday evening, I turned to Debbie to tell her I needed to call Larry and tell him to bring his wine decanter. The get-togethers with his family and others always meant some wine tasting and more. I don't know why I thought of him at that moment, three days before our scheduled get-together, but I did. Now I know why. It was just a few minutes later when the house phone rang and our friend Adam Oberfeld broke the news, Larry was gone, hit and killed while riding his road bike that afternoon.

I'm here to tell you as sure as I feel it today, more than four years later, his spirit passed right through that screened-in porch where my family was having dinner that evening. It was the reason I suddenly thought about him, and minutes later, learned of his passing.

From that moment, I felt Larry had reached out to me, passed right through, made me think about him and shortly thereafter, I was on a mission. Over the next year plus, I reached out to Tami as much as possible through texts and e-mails trying to help her cope with a loss which was unimaginable and was draining the strength from her very soul. Every time she shared her heart-wrenching experiences of loss, I tried to fight back to somehow lift her spirits with messages of hope, messages about life, messages about perseverance, messages about taking it one step and one day at a time. I kept telling Tami one day, one day, she would be able to breathe again. All along I felt Larry with me, guiding me, asking me to reach out and to make sure his girls would be OK. You never get over it, you just get on with it. The ultimate goal: to keep moving forward.

Fast forward to today. This is the 5th annual Larry's Ride, a ride for cyclists to come and take to the roads over four challenging routes, to raise money to help advance the advocacy efforts of Bike Maryland, a non-profit dedicated to promoting bicycling, increasing safety, improving conditions and providing a voice for all bicyclists in Maryland, (https://www.bikemaryland.org/). It was Tami and friends who came up with the idea for the event and it was Tami, who just days after Larry's death, helped to push through legislation to create the 3-foot-rule for drivers when passing cyclists on the roads in Maryland.

And now it's time...the same time which seemed to stand still after Larry was killed, but now moves along at a more normal pace for the Bensky family. "I guess we are doing great," says Tami. "We still have all the family and friends supporting us as well as solid community support, our school and the Beth El congregation. What is cool is we are frequently talking about Larry. Just last night, Kate was acting goofy and my mom came up to her and said to her, 'you are such your father's daughter.' It was an innocent comment which just a few years earlier brought pain and an unbearable sense of loss, now it brings about laughter and warm memories.

When someone you love becomes a memory, that memory becomes a treasure. Today Larry's daughters, Gabi and Kate, as well as many of their friends will be cheering on other cyclists and the memory of their Dad as hundreds ride in his honor and cross the finish line at Larry's Ride. In these five years the Ride has raised more than $100,000, a tribute to Tami's dedication, along with a legion of friends and supporters to keep the event going and those who turn out to participate.

Larry Bensky did so many things for others, for family, for friends, for business associates. He shared his wisdom, his insight, his hard work, even dollars from his own pocket and the clothes off his back to help a friend in need. He was living proof of the words I recently heard – a day without doing something good is a day without truly living.

And I'm going to repeat something I read and shared when I first wrote about Larry more than a year ago on this blog, because it is not only powerful, but I believe helps to truly define the kind of man Larry was and the spirit he possessed. The passage is from a book titled *Put Your Dream to the Test*, by John Maxwell: *"A rare minority of people are able to hold closely to their dream to make a difference and are willing to give up everything to make that dream come true. Of people like that, it will never be said that when they died, it was as though they never lived."*

I underlined the passage in that book and wrote one word next to it... Larry.

Until next time, thanks for taking the time.

The Sunday Series: The Lucky One

It all began with a small bump on the head, one which Neha says she believed was nothing - maybe she bumped her head on her headboard while she was sleeping. What Neha couldn't know then, from head to toe, her life would be forever changed.

—Mark Brodinsky

They say the journey of a thousand miles begins with one small step. For Neha Kundagrami the steps are painful, yet through it all, she keeps the faith, keeps her head up, believes she is one of the lucky ones. It all began with a small bump on the head, one which Neha says she believed was nothing – maybe she bumped her head on her headboard while she was sleeping. What Neha couldn't know then, that from head to toe, her life would be forever changed.

"I kind of ignored the bump at first," says Neha. "Then it started getting bigger and bigger. We started going to different doctors and the frightening thing was no two doctors concurred and every one said something different." When some swelling also began on her neck, Neha and her family finally visited a head and neck surgeon and he referred them to someone from his graduating class who worked at Johns Hopkins Pediatric Oncology. A lymph node was extracted. The diagnosis: Acute B Cell Lymphoblastic Lymphoma. Lymphoma is the most common blood cancer. Cancerous lymphocytes can travel to many parts of the body and can accumulate to form tumors. Some of the most common forms of treatment are chemotherapy and steroids, but these treatments take their toll.

"This has probably been the hardest on my family and my parents watching me go through this, watching me go through chemo is the only time I ever saw my Dad cry. Plus I have always been deathly afraid of needles. Even at the age of 16, I had to hold my mother's hand while getting a blood test done, often while choking back tears. So it was with the deepest sense of irony that, (at the age of 16), I was diagnosed with cancer, a diagnosis that inevitably comes with a guarantee of the patient turning into a human pincushion."

But then there's the other side effect of chemotherapy which Neha so eloquently explains: "No one understands what it's like to be a kid with cancer. Ask any cancer patient what the worst part of chemotherapy is and they will not list any of the drugs that they had to take, or any pill, radiation or medication of some sort. Chemo is hard, but it is necessary, it becomes bearable. For almost all the patients the worst part of chemotherapy is the isolation it forces. The patient is forced to spend months at a time either at home or in the hospital, barred from civilization. Without the common distractions, such as a trip to the movies, a day at an amusement park, or even something as simple as having friends over, there is nothing to distract from the discomfort of cancer treatment, which somehow manages to make the treatment even worse."

But it was visits and spending time at places like Camp Sunrise, the camp for child cancer patients, which gave Neha hope and the realization she was not the only one. Neha saw all these other children going through the same lonely disease she was: "They are kids, but they still managed to be kids despite the cancer, so there is no reason I can't be."

At the age of 19, Neha is now finished with the chemotherapy and the steroid treatments which saved her life. But its hold on her life is far from over. Neha describes her journey into cancer as a "long, dark tunnel," and it took baby steps to realize she could make it through, but the reality of those steps became increasingly more painful. The steroid treatments affected her mobility – in a big way. Her left hip collapsed and cannot be saved. Neha says, "imagine taking a ping-pong ball and running it over with a tractor and then putting it back in. That's what my hip joint is like, flat." A recent surgery, a bone graft on her right hip has stopped that disintegration. But now Neha moves about her college campus on crutches, not the easiest of travels and walking will be about the most she will ever be able to do – no running, no jumping, no dancing – just walking – the simple ability to get from one place to another. Yet Neha believes she is lucky.

"For so many kids cancer is their lives, it becomes their lives," says Neha. "There are cancer patients that will never walk across the stage at graduation, never go to college, never get married or have kids. I'm one of the lucky ones. Two of my friends, Brooke Lauren Shockley and Sarah McMohan weren't as lucky. They didn't make it. After all the radiation, surgeries, chemo, spinal taps, and hospital visits –nothing worked. They passed away before they even had a chance to live, and were stripped of their lives and their potential from the raging monster of cancer. These kids are the next generation, and every one of them deserves a chance at life. I can't do anything about the suffering cancer has put me through. I can't do anything about the scars it left, or the year I lost to treatment, or the months spent in the hospital begging to go home. But I can work to see the end of cancer. I can work to find a cure, so that children like Sarah and Brooke have the chance to grow past their teenage years and so that no mother goes home to an empty bedroom where her baby once slept. Because you can't change the cards life handed you, but you can change how you play the hand."

Neha is taking the hand she has been dealt and doing all she can to live a so-called normal existence. It's been a long journey out of her tunnel to see the light. But it is this light which kept her moving forward. "I remember after I was diagnosed," says Neha, "I was told I would be bald, and couldn't go to school and I collapsed and started bawling. I remember looking up and it was cloudy and stormy, but five minutes later I took a break from crying and I remember looking up again and it was sunny with no clouds in sight. I remember thinking that today might suck, but my future is so bright. I am one of the lucky ones, I realize that now. I may have had more surgeries than I care to remember. I may have had so many tubes sprouting from me that I looked like a blossoming flower. I may have even been so sick I couldn't even remember what being healthy actually felt like. But I had a cure, a chance to get my life back. I had hope."

THE SUNDAY SERIES WITH MARK BRODINSKY

And hope is far from overrated. Sometimes it's all you have. As the calendar turns from National Childhood Cancer Awareness Month, for so many children with cancer, time seems to stand still. Neha believes so many more advances can be made to better the lives of children fighting to survive. "Cancer advances happen every day", says Neha. "Targeted gene therapy, nanobots and other new, less painful ways of treating cancer are being discovered every day. But work still remains. There are still cancers for which there is no cure, or cancers for which the success rate is far lower than we would like. And we cannot rest until every cancer has a simple, easy cure, for our job will not be done until no other child has to suffer."

No more suffering. A chance to become one of the "lucky ones", like Neha. It's a chance worth fighting for.

Until next time, thanks for taking the time.

The Sunday Series: Madelyn Backstage

Mark wrote a Sunday Series about my daughter Madelyn. She has a disease called Gaucher, which means she is lacking an enzyme and needs bi-weekly infusions. She started when she was 8 and is now 15. She will need these infusions for the rest of her life.

Mark wrote a story about Madelyn explaining her situation, making it easy for everyone to understand. He highlighted Madelyn's strengths and made her feel proud when she read it. He helped spread the word about a disease that is not well known and brought much needed awareness. Mark also inspired so much pride and recognition for Madelyn - acknowledging her courageous way of dealing with Gaucher. Our whole family is grateful for Mark and his natural talent to share people's stories with the world.

–Jenny Schloss

She seemed almost too perfect: dark black hair, perfect skin, deep blue eyes. A beautiful baby girl – stunning. "Everyone said I should do something with her," says her mom, Jenny Schloss. "My sister, a writer and producer in LA, guided me on how to get an agent. We got an agent in New York when Madelyn was only five-months-old. Her first audition was for the cover of *American Baby* magazine. Out of 100 babies, Madelyn was one of two to get the callback. I was in hook, line and sinker,"says Jenny. Less than half-a-year on this earth and Madelyn's modeling/acting career was on its way...only challenge was the publishers of *American Baby* chose two babies in case one didn't cooperate for the photo shoot, Madelyn was the one who didn't cooperate. Gig over. But Madelyn still got booked and got paid. At five months of age, a star was born.

A few years later that star began to flicker.

Jenny and her husband Adam had planned a weekend trip to Atlantic City, to stay at the new Borgata hotel and casino. Jenny was rushing around with last-minute plans, and so she barely had time to take Madelyn to the pediatrician to check out the cough she had been fighting for some time. Jenny says Dr. Rona Stein laid Madelyn down to feel her stomach. Feel her stomach? For a cough? Dr. Stein was just being thorough she said.

The extra touch proved to be a life-saver.

Dr. Stein said there was something about Madelyn's spleen, it didn't feel right and she told Jenny to take her daughter to get an ultrasound. Jenny admits it wasn't her best day...she immediately thought the worst –"was it the C word?" There was no way to be sure until a test was done. They immediately headed for the ultrasound which showed Madelyn's spleen and liver were enlarged, but, as Jenny puts it, "the good news was there were no tumors." A fun weekend on the horizon in Atlantic City was now taking a backseat to a medical mystery consisting of tests and uncertainty surrounding her baby girl.

Now the attention turned to figuring out what Madelyn's condition might be –enlarged spleen and liver, her blood platelets "off"– the family met with Dr. Joseph Wiley at Sinai Hospital in Baltimore who quickly gave them the diagnosis, Gaucher Disease. "It's not possible," said Jenny, "I'm not a carrier." Gaucher Disease results from a specific enzyme deficiency in the body, caused by a genetic mutation received from both parents. It is also the most common genetic disease affecting Ashkenazi Jewish people with a carrier frequency of 1-in-10 affected. Jenny and Adam had both been tested before Madelyn was born and only Adam had been identified as a carrier, one parent, not both. Jenny says. "I told the doctor he was wrong."

But Dr. Wiley had no doubt. When Jenny was tested pre-pregnancy, it showed she could be a carrier of cystic fibrosis, but perhaps there had been a mistake. Whatever the genesis, the present results were clear, Madelyn had Gaucher Disease. At first, the doctor said he didn't believe the disease has affected Madelyn's bones, and because Madelyn was so young, they could wait about a year to begin infusions. But an MRI was scheduled and the results surprised even the doctor– the disease was in Madelyn's bones, at least a little – and he recommended infusions begin immediately. (Madelyn's brother Jake, who was born before Madelyn was diagnosed and tested, does not have the disease.)

Gaucher Disease can involve many organ systems, such as liver, spleen, lungs, brain, metabolism and bone marrow. It is also broken down into three subtypes according to the presence or absence of neurological involvement. Fortunately for Madelyn, the disease was Type 1 and there was no sign of neurological trauma, but others are not so lucky. Types 2 and 3 can cause severe trauma and even death. For 6-year-old Madelyn the treatment would be the infusion of Cerezyme, basically a drug to replace the enzyme she was lacking which kept her liver, spleen and platelets in order. (http://www.gaucherdisease.org/)

Jenny says she still recalls her fear and anxiety, calling friends and fearing the worst, her daughter had a disease for which she would need infusions for the rest of her life! Adam took the other road, for too many the one less traveled, but the one which brings calm and certainty to handling any disease – Adam did the research, learned about the treatments, knew it was caught early and was ready to accept that fact Madelyn had Gaucher, but would be OK.

That was of course until the first infusion. It was Adam who held his daughter in his arms for that first infusion at Sinai Hospital, held her tight as the needle went into her veins and the tears started to flow.

After the first few infusions at the hospital, which needed to happen every two weeks, the treatments got a bit easier. The infusions, which have varied in frequency from two weeks apart to three to even four, are now back to a two-week span, since Madelyn, at age 13, is now going through puberty and the doctor believes with all those changes, more frequent treatments are beneficial.

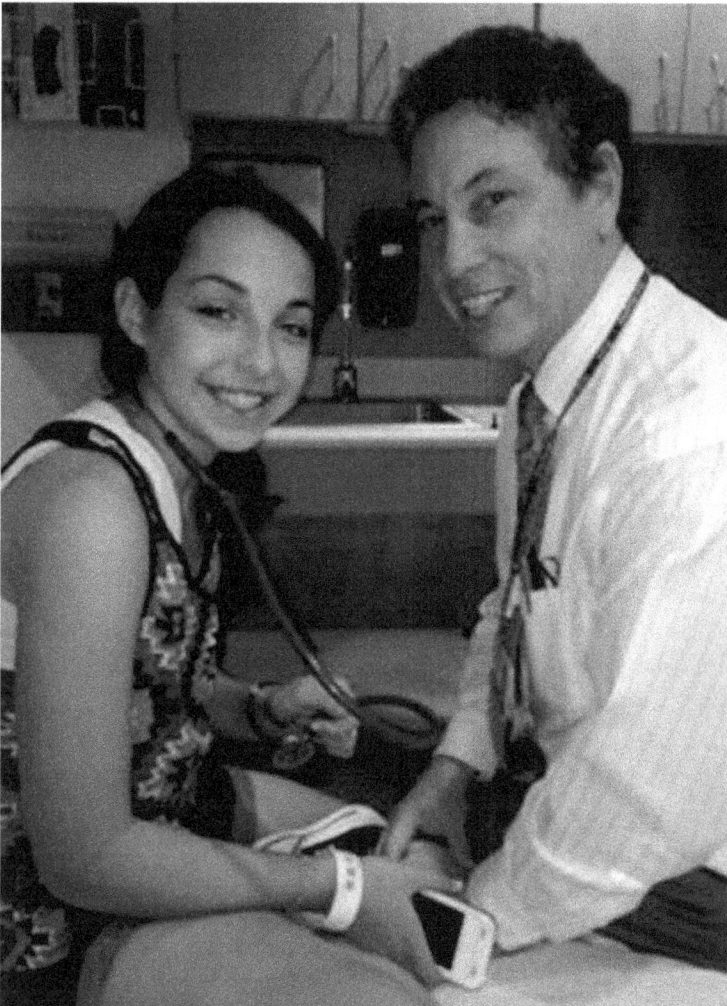

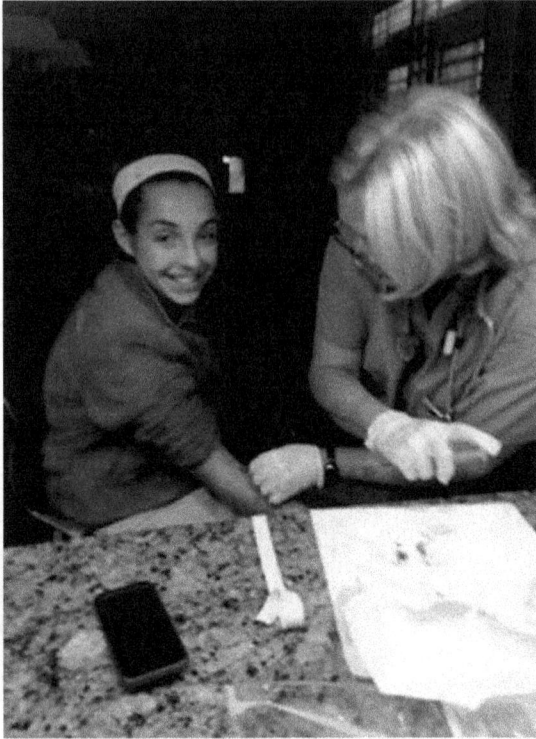

But the infusions have their own story. When any child is sick, it's a sick feeling for those who love her or him the most, their family and friends. And it's Jenny's long-time friends who have been the beacon of light for Madelyn since the time the day the very first needle was injected. The friends, many of whom Jenny has known since she herself was a little girl, do a round-robin, bringing Madelyn a gift for EVERY infusion, never missing a beat. Early on Jenny says she would hold up the gift right at the moment the needle was going into Madelyn's vein, just to serve as a distraction. Even now, as Madelyn begins her teenage years, the gifts keep on coming. And Jenny says it still makes a difference. There's something about the knowledge others care, which never grows old, even as you do.

The support of an entire community has been on full display as well for Madelyn, and for all those children who have Gaucher. A few years ago the family held a Go for Gaucher event, a walk/run which raised $70,000 for the National Gaucher Foundation. And maybe just as important as the money raised, was the show of support – 450 people – many of them volunteers – participated in the event, proving once again, it takes a village to help raise a child, especially when those children are in need.

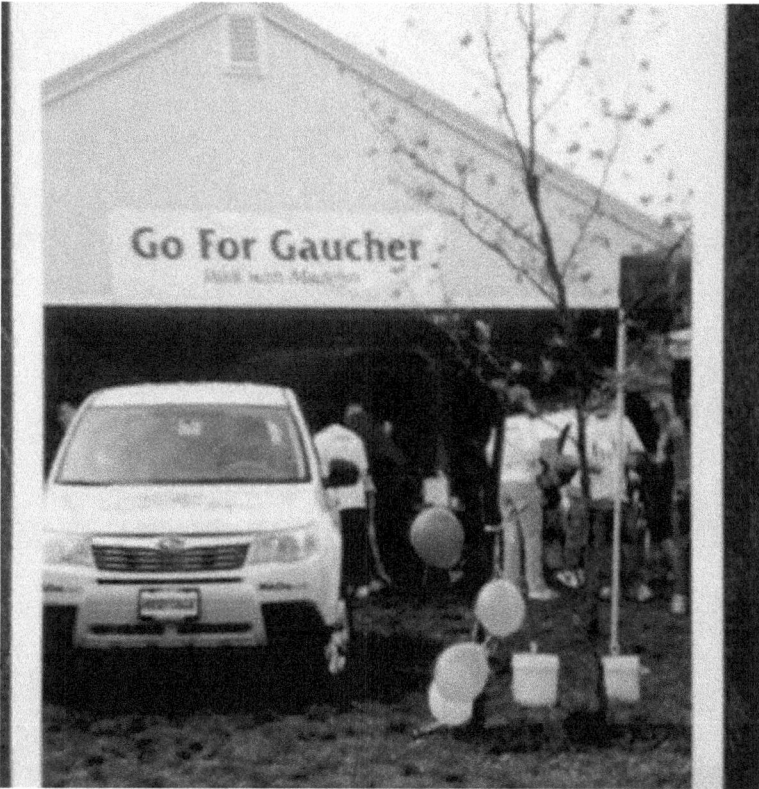

And it's Madelyn, who, surrounded by those ready to help her at a moment's notice, has learned the meaning of the word "give." Madelyn has connected with other children also dealing with the disease through Skype chats, even talking to a 6-year-old girl while the young lady was getting her infusion– providing a show of support and a sense of calm and maybe most importantly hope, from a beautiful, vibrant 13-year-old who shares the same disease, but was telling her all would be OK.

For Madelyn, showing the world you can shine, despite any obstacle, or distraction, has become a daily part of her world. Since that first baby photo shoot went south 13 years ago, Madelyn has experienced plenty of success: modeling, acting, singing and showing the whole world how she can shine.

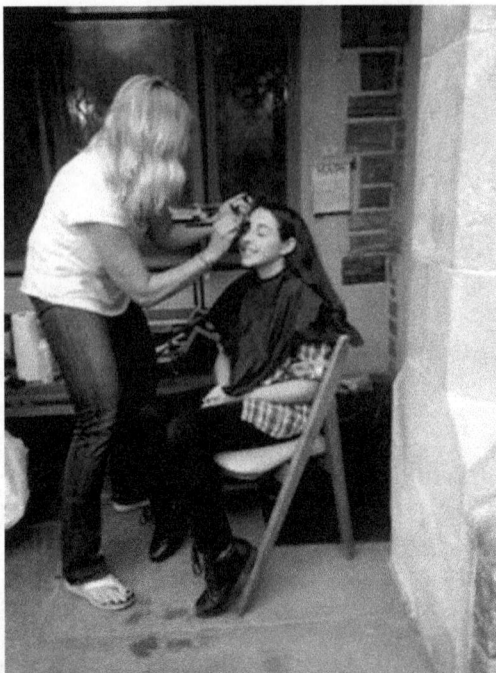

Yet despite all the success and the accolades which come with the bright lights of the stage, video and television, it might be the performance that only a few got to see last year, which is her shining moment so far. Jenny was kind enough to provide me with the speech Madelyn gave to her 7th grade class during something called Survival Week, (the speech is included below). Other people visited the class to talk about experiences they survived or endured, but Madelyn was the only classmate to get up and to share the experience she has lived since she was 6 years of age and will continue to live with for the rest of her life. It is permanent proof that Madelyn gets it. She knows that behind the curtain of all her success, the backstage of her life helps determine her front stage, and it has made her a stronger, more grounded individual, understanding what makes life important and gives it meaning is how you overcome, how you survive and live to shine.

Madelyn's speech:

"The theme of this week is survival. The interesting thing about survival is that each and every one of us deals with survival in some way. Whether it's how we survive a physical challenge, a dangerous situation or even how we deal with a simple everyday sort of problem. The bottom line is that we are faced with some sort of obstacle and we have to choose how we are going to get through it.

When I was six years old, I was told I had Gaucher Disease. It's a rare genetic disorder in which I am lacking a certain enzyme that I cannot even attempt to pronounce. My platelet count was low, my spleen and liver were enlarged and the Gaucher cells were starting to invade my bones. Dr. Wiley at Sinai Hospital said that I would have to get 2-hour infusions every two weeks to replace the enzyme that I am lacking. For the rest of my life. There were blood test, ultrasounds and MRIs. And soon after was my first infusion at Sinai Hospital. Eventually, we arranged for a nurse to come to our home to do the infusions. It has been six years since my diagnosis. Now every two weeks my nurse, Karen comes to my house and every three months I go to Sinai for my infusion along with blood work and other tests. I guess the whole thing could be kind of annoying. I mean who wants to get a needle every two weeks for their entire life? And then have to sit hooked up to an IV pump for two hours? And who likes blood tests or loud MRIs that you have to lay still inside a tube for 45 minutes?

One thing that I learned through this whole ordeal is that everything is relative. I get my infusions in the pediatric oncology department at Sinai. I see many children who lost all their hair getting chemo for their cancer. Most of them are actually upbeat, usually accompanied by their parents doing what they have to do to get better and survive.

Some of my closest friends have food allergies. They struggle everyday always being cautious with every morsel of food that goes into their mouths. They read every ingredient on what they eat and ask waiters in restaurants all the right questions. They are always prepared with an EpiPen nearby just in case. They take precautions and educate themselves with the knowledge necessary to continue to lead a healthy life and survive.

Most of my friends are lucky and do not have to deal with serious health issues. But I have friends who deal with other issues. Some struggle with family problems. Some have trouble focusing on their schoolwork and some have difficult situations with friends.

The bottom line is that we all have struggles. The most important thing about that is how do we survive our struggles? When I get my infusions, I always have something in front of me to keep my mind occupied. Whether I'm studying for a Hebrew test or watching Pretty Little Liars.

My mom has a group of friends who have been close since high school. All eight girls have a schedule where they alternate bringing me some sort of gift for every infusion for the past six years! As soon as Karen puts the needle in my arm, there's a present sitting in front of me. These girls literally made me look forward to my infusions instead of dreading them.

After I was diagnosed, my family, friends and I organized a "Go for Gaucher" walk to raise money and awareness for Gaucher disease. So many of you were there and helped us to raise $70,000 for the Gaucher Foundation. It felt so good to sort of get up and do something to fight this disease instead of letting it get me down.

I also am in touch with other Gaucher patients through friends and social media. I speak to other children who have been recently diagnosed and give them advice on dealing with the disease.

We will hear all different stories of survival this week. I am sure we will be inspired by each one. I know I am inspired by all the people around me who deal with their own issues. I hope I can help by sharing my story. I think the best way to get through something is to first accept it. Then figure out what you can do to not only get through it but do more than that. Figure out how you can turn a negative situation into a positive one. A way to maybe help yourself get through and even help others along the way. We all can do it. Survive any obstacle. But even better persevere!

Until next time, thanks for taking the time.

The Sunday Series: A Man of Good Hope

Thirty seconds after Mark contacted me I knew I found my voice. Although he knew very little about the rare cancer I had, he took the time to research it and understand my story. What can I say? He transformed the words I gave him into a story that touches hearts, and still brings tears to my eyes every time I read it. His weekly Sunday Series stories keep my fire burning to help others find hope in their struggle with rare diseases.

–Rich Mosca

Neil had passed away and it was a crushing blow. It happens way too often these days, but it was another of those moments Richard realized what this is really all about. "I went to visit Neil's wife after he was gone," says Richard. "She put her arm around me and revealed to me what Neil had said about me – he told her, 'I met this guy, he is a long-time survivor and talking to him... he gives me hope.' My knees almost buckled and I started to cry."

It's a moment Richard Mosca will long remember. And there have been so many more. It's a sacrifice Richard makes to be a savior to so many on their journey. It's not easy, because how many times can you lose a friend? How many times can a heart break? Apparently, many more times than Richard realized he could handle, but the sacrifice of emotional pain is worth it, if even one soul can live a day of hope.

For Richard, it all began with some night sweats. He thought it was simply a complication from the diverticulitis he had dealt with for years. A little bloating, drenched sheets, par for the course. Even at his annual physical in October of 2006, he failed to mention it, until the end of the appointment. When the doctor asked Richard if there was anything else he wanted to talk about, Richard shared his recent symptoms, the doctor raised his eyebrows... then sent him off for a CAT scan. The journey had begun.

Throughout the winter of 2006, a series of tests, surgery on Richard's abdomen, a blood clot in his neck, lymph nodes removed, another round of abdomen surgery —finally some clarity. The winter of Richard's discontent had finally landed him on the doorstep of an oncologist at Columbia Presbyterian Hospital in New York. This doctor, a specialist, recommended one more biopsy. A 10-inch piece of Richard's omentum was removed, (omentum is the skin which hangs just above the abdomen), and it was sent off for testing. The result: mesothelioma, an aggressive cancer affecting the membrane lining of the lungs and abdomen. The abdominal "meso" affects only about 600 people a year in the United States, rare enough that funding is hard to come by for research and patient advocacy. The primary cause for mesothelioma – exposure to asbestos. And understand this fact: Asbestos kills more people than road traffic accidents every year. Inhaling the fibers can cause the cancer mesothelioma to develop as much *as half a century after exposure.*

For Richard, he is fairly certain he came in contact with the asbestos while employed, but explains there are plenty of ways to contract the disease and it's not always primary contact. A woman who has become Richard's mentor contracted the disease from secondary exposure. The woman's father, who worked as an electrician while she was growing up, was exposed to asbestos nearly every day. When he came home, her father would routinely take off his work clothes and leave them in the laundry room *—the same room which also served as a playroom for his children.* It is this same woman who helped Richard a great deal, especially as he was going through his rounds of chemotherapy following the first surgery. Richard remembers thinking, "I want to be just like her," giving hope to those scared to death of what lies ahead.

Often it's not the fear of surgery, but simply survival which gnaws at the heart. Richard's greatest fears following his two surgeries in 2007 were if he would make it – what if he was not there to walk his daughter down the aisle – and wondering if he were gone tomorrow would his young grandchildren still remember him.

"With cancer you just never know,", says Richard. "All could be great, then six months later it recurs, you just don't know. The doctors said I had a more aggressive tumor than they wanted to see. Now every time there is a little pain or something doesn't feel right you start to think, oh crap, it's back."

But Richard is one of the lucky ones. Mesothelioma doesn't play games. One-third of all meso patients don't last a year, another third of patients see their cancer return in five years and only one-third manage to live beyond five years. And it's not just survival, it's the games a serious illness can play with your mind. Richard was fortunate enough to have a large amount of sick time from his job at Con Edison in New York City, but now looks back and wonders if that was a big mistake. "I found myself sitting around the house and obsessing with this," Richard says. "I would research mesothelioma on the internet and only saw negativity– all the law firms telling you to get a lawyer, (for what so many refer to as the TV cancer, with all the mesothelioma commercials out there), and people seeking holistic approaches and not using chemotherapy. I started to wonder if I was going to regret my route of treatment. It became a mental nightmare. My wife would come home and I would be in the same position on the couch as when she left me. I found myself getting depressed without even realizing it. I would sit there and not care about anything."

It was Richard's wife Lora, who saw the signs and turned things around. "My wife recognized the depression and soon gave me things to do. She made sure when she left in the morning for work, I had errands to run, I would go visit people or even go to the library, sit down and read for a while. She kept her eye on me and in a round-a-bout way kept me busy without being direct about the depression."

CAT scans and checks are a way of life now, but it was 3½ years after Richard's second surgery, when Richard thought it was all over. "After looking at my CAT scan, the doctor walks right over to me, sits down in front of me and says, 'you have a mass on the right side of your abdomen.' I was almost sure it had come back. At that point I had made it further than I thought I would," says Richard. But luck was on his side, because the mass was removed, tested and it turned out it was just an infection from Richard's diverticulitis, not a return of the cancer. It's now been two years since that most recent false alarm... and Richard continues to move forward on his mission to bring hope to other meso victims.

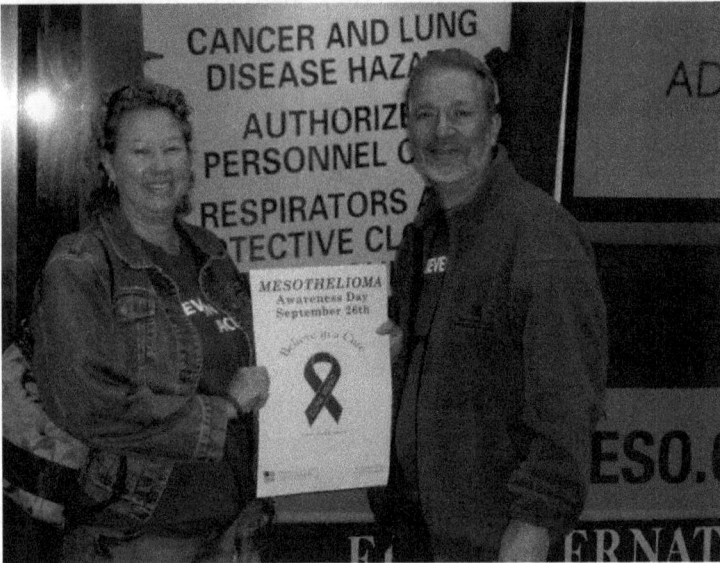

"I'm big into the (Mesothelioma Applied Research) Foundation, (http://www.curemeso.org/site/c.duIWJfNQKiL8G/b.8598593/k.D685/Homepage.htm). I served on the Board for three years, but now I'm off the Board because they want me to become the face of the Foundation. One of Richard's notable efforts to bring mesothelioma to the forefront of people's minds resulted in an official proclamation in the State of New York, declaring September 26th, "Mesothelioma Awareness Day."

For seven years now Richard has been an active member of the mesothelioma patient community and through a nomination by the Mesothelioma Applied Research Foundation, he has participated in six congressionally directed medical research grant panels, giving him a unique perspective that most patients do not experience. But it IS the patient experience to which Richard can mostly closely relate and the one he is living to change: (https://www.facebook.com/curemeso)

It's not easy because the pain of loss permeates Richard's life, it's something he has learned to live with since early on in the journey. "I'm a big Yankee fan," says Richard. "When I went to my first chemotherapy session I wore all my Yankee stuff. The guy in the chair next to me, David, was decked out in Red Sox gear, but we became the best of friends. We would jab at each other a lot about each team. David would come in frequently for treatment because he had it (meso) bad. We spent a lot of time together. I would go pick him up and take him out to dinner. He was one of the good guys. I remember the Giants-Patriots Super Bowl and when the Giants won, David still called me up to congratulate me. We were sports enemies, but we were the best of friends. When David passed, he wrote his wife a note and she read it at the funeral."

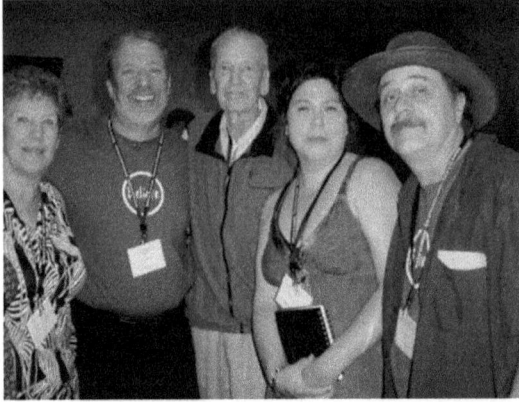

Too many funerals, too many losses. But Richard says he gets so much satisfaction out of making the connections. "I have the nurse match me with new patients about my age, she gets me in contact with them and I allow them to pick my brain. I don't sugar-coat it. I tell them how I survived, what I went through and what they can do to try to avoid the pain, little tricks that help. I tell them how I was swinging my golf clubs six weeks after surgery. I always, always stay positive."

Richard and Lora don't just open their hearts, they even open the door to their home. "Other things we do to help is offer our home up to people who are coming to New York for treatments. Their family or caregivers can stay with us as long as they require." It's finding a way to bring some hope. While Richard may not be able to change the final outcome for others dealing with mesothelioma, he can try to bring joy to the journey. Even one day of hope is better than none at all.

And then there's the takeaway so many dealing with a serious illness find – life is precious. "I tell everyone to appreciate your friends and family," says Richard. "And the biggest thing I tell everyone is even if you are going through bad experiences you must live today and worry about tomorrow when it gets here. It's the way I live my life now. Worry about today because it's here, it's important. Tomorrow is another day."

Another day of good hope.

Until next time, thanks for taking the time.

The Sunday Series: Wealth Is Health

I loved sharing my story with Mark because he listened to what I said and understood the impact my story had on my life. I never realized that living through the death of my brother and now losing weight and getting healthy would inspire others. A big part of that was the effort Mark Brodinsky made to tell my story with accuracy and love. It meant the world to me that he takes the spoken word to create a beautiful, relatable story. I felt so honored that he chose my story to highlight in his Sunday Series.

–Lesley Bogash

More than 70,000 people on their feet, shouting, screaming, going crazy, loving life and every moment of what they are witnessing down on the field at the Ravens game. But one football fan found this hard to believe. Lesley Winer Bogash couldn't understand how 70,000 other people could seem so happy, so carefree. Was it that she was the only one who felt differently? How come her heart wasn't as full of joy, her energy not at the same level, her enthusiasm not just for the game, but for life, not where she thought it should be. And how could it be that all these people seemed to be having the time of their lives, while she felt anxious and afraid?

When you're not where you want to be in life, your mind can play tricks on you, making it seem as if everyone else is happy and fulfilled. It's not the truth, far from it, but sometimes, it's all in the way you choose to see life.

Twenty-four years ago life changed for Lesley in a dramatic fashion. Her big brother Andy, at the young age of 22, succumbed to a rare type of cancer. When Andy died, a part of Lesley went with him. "I idolized Andy," says Lesley. "He was a good big brother, he looked after me. He enjoyed me being his sister. He had a zest for life. If it was winter he wanted to ski, if it was summer he wanted to be at the beach, his zest for life was incredible.

I lost that when he died. He made me brave. I suffered from anxiety until this year. And then I had an *a-ha!*– which was when I realized I was trying to fill the void in my life from my brother's loss, with something…that something was food."

Part of that realization came to light about six months ago, when Lesley decided to attend a 2-day workshop her friend Tracey was teaching at Stevenson University: *Defining Your Dependable Strength*. It was the beginning of a new beginning. A questionnaire she filled out during the workshop made her recognize a life-changing philosophy: "everything I had been doing for 20 years, I didn't really like," says Lesley. "Everything the survey said I should be doing I wasn't and everything it said I shouldn't be doing I was. It was a good eye-opener."

That workshop, along with her entry into her latest weight loss program, the courage to leave a job she says was making her miserable, "because it wasn't the right fit for me," and reading more spiritual and inspirational books, ended up creating the perfect storm for change in Lesley's life. "The end of June I went on this weight loss program and it opened my mind to other things and I loved it. I decided to try it for one month. I've been on diets for 20 years and always got close to the goal and failed. I also quit my job before having another, because of my health. It was making me so unhappy. One day you have to get up and say this is not for me and move on to do what you love. When I walked away, it was scary to do. I went on a mission to find a job that suits me and not make it just about the money. I also started reading a lot of self-help and spiritual books."

It all made a difference. Lesley lost 45 pounds and the weight loss/coaching program inspired Lesley to do this for others – she became a health coach - then took a course to get certified through the MacDonald Center for Obesity Prevention and Education, (http://www1.villanova.edu/villanova/nursing/centers/obesity.html). "I've been on every diet known to man," says Lesley, "but this program, the way it's set up, it's easy. I call it the diet for dummies, because it's so simple. For the program I am on, you get clients through word of mouth and on social media. They just pay for the food. I have 15 clients right now. I talk to them twice a week, help them through their struggles, psychological and physical. Healthy body, healthy mind, healthy finances. If you have all three, you are leading a pretty good life." (http://yourbestself.ichooseoptimalhealth.com/)

"It's not just about losing weight. Any program you are on, you are probably going to lose weight. It's the one-to-one interaction that changes everything because you are more likely to take action and to change. I like that because it's honest. On this program I really concentrate on health. If I choose health, then I'm not eating things that are bad for me. Every diet I've ever been on I would have this dream about eating a one-pound bag of M&M's....really. Not this time."

Lesley has also come to learn that good health and helping others is her passion. "I'm helping a woman who was over 300 pounds and she is doing amazing," says Lesley. And it's not just about the weight, it's the mindset. "I have a client who is a lawyer and because of how she now looks and thinks, she feels more confident when she goes into the courtroom. My best friend Patti, who has been my best friend since we were little, decided to join me as well. She has been successful in her career and monetarily, but she has been battling this weight demon, and now she has lost 30 pounds and we are both in a better place. Patti told me I've got my groove back, she would know because she knows how much I suffered when my brother died."

It's all about mindset. Mind over body. Mind over anything really. It's the attitude you carry into every situation that can change your life and attract others who then want to be around you. And Lesley says this time, it's for real. She says she used to post positive quotes on Facebook, but one day her friend called her out on it. Lesley says, "she told me you are posting these quotes you don't really believe, you aren't living it. But now what I post, I really believe I am living it. Now I don't feel fraudulent in anything I say. I don't put up anything I don't believe in. I wouldn't be a successful health coach if I didn't believe in the program or in myself. I was always charitable, but I never realized how helping other people makes such a difference...that's what everything is about!"

If you change, things change for you. Believe with all your heart you can and you will. Lesley has now used this to overcome maybe her greatest temptation –chocolate. For 15 years she has run a chocolate business out of her home called "So Delish." She still does this and every day she is surrounded by the sweet, delicious temptation of her own creations, but it's her new thought process and philosophy which has stopped her from continuing to sample the chocolate. "I feel so healthy and so good I want other people suffering to feel like I do now. It feels good to help people. It's better than any piece of chocolate I ever put in my mouth."

And so check chocolate off the list, replace it with a health coach making a difference. If you change, things change for you.

And the changes keep coming. Lesley says when she told her husband Ryan she was going into this program, he couldn't believe she was going on yet another diet. But he agreed to let her try it and Lesley says, "because I am so much happier, we are getting along better." Others are noticing the new Lesley as well. Her 14-year-old son Alec is usually way more interested in his friends and his phone than what his mother is doing, but just recently he told her how proud he is of her and how she is helping other people. "It brought tears to my eyes," says Lesley, "and made me proud of myself. When you are proud of yourself you walk around differently. When I take a walk the colors bombard me, they didn't before. Now I'm taking it (life) in, I feel like a blind person who just had surgery and now I'm not blind anymore."

Lesley is no longer just a big Ravens fan, she is a fan of life. In our conversation for this blog, Lesley and I had tremendous synergy in our thought process and philosophy, and her greatest takeaway from what she is witnessing this past year is the same as mine. She says, "the biggest thing is to stop waiting for your life to begin. I waited 24 years for my life to begin. Stop waiting and stop thinking, 'when I get this age I will have this, or when I'm this thin I will get to do this'...every day I have something fun now. Live your life and live it to the fullest you can possibly live it. I'm in the moment now, I live in the moment. I always heard the expression, but now I live it. And I have a whole life to live before the next moment. Don't keep waiting for the next moment to happen. Find a new way."

Not only has Lesley found a new way – but she can now answer her life's most important question – the one she has asked herself over and over again since she lost her best friend – her brother – more than 20 years ago. "I always asked myself, would Andy be proud of me? This year I can ask myself that question and answer, yeah, he would have been proud."

Until next time, thanks for taking the time.

The Sunday Series: A Reason To Believe

So don't yield to the fortunes you sometimes see as fate, they may have a new perspective on a different day. And if you don't give up and don't give in it may just be OK.

—The Living Years, by Mike & The Mechanics

There is meaning and purpose to your life. There is hope for tomorrow and there is something you can follow and dream after, so don't give up.

—Alex Penduck

Sometimes all it takes is a little faith.

For Alex and Raquel Penduck, it began with conversations outside on the deck of their condominium. The talks were about what they could see all around them. People in their 20's and 30's getting married, getting the house, getting the cars, having the kids, going to work, coming home, the same routine over and over with no real connection to a community or a place of faith. And when problems or issues would arise, there was no place to turn to work it out. Alex and Raquel knew these people, just like themselves, needed direction, a place to go, a way to connect, a reason to believe.

The couple knows from faith and the challenges and the disconnect others in their age group feel. Alex, originally from England and Raquel, born in Nicaragua, met in the summer of 2000 in Springfield, Missouri. They eventually married a few years later and moved to Maryland. For a while they worked on the staff of a fairly large church, a church struggling to survive. Alex says the challenges for that church, as well as others, are many. What we had seen and observed, says Alex, a lot of people thought the church was an ugly place, they really didn't care about them, we started hearing that a lot. People had been hurt by the church, they had been taken advantage of, people said things in trust and confidence and that trust had been broken. They felt the church used them for what it could get out of them and not give anything back. And as we looked around we noticed a void, where were all the twenty and thirty somethings, the people just like us?

Alex and Raquel believed that those just like them, just starting out, raising young families, dealing with family and marital issues needed hope and faith and a connection to church and community, but they had nowhere to turn and no place to go.

For the young couple, the conversations outside their condo in 2009 were all about these issues and how they could find a way to fill the void. How they could develop a sense of community, a safe haven, a place where these young families wanted to go to gather, talk through the issues, reconnect with their faith and to find hope. The young couple soon brought their friends into the conversation and the dream started to take shape. There were only eight of them, talking in the living room of a friend's home – brainstorming and dreaming about how they could create a place where people would want to come – what a church might look like – what issues were most important. How could they help to heal broken marriages, help others to understand who God truly is, understand faith and provide a place where people could experience love. How could they take what they saw as surface relationships to a deeper place where you could trust and really love other people.

On September 19th, 2010, Generation Church became a reality. Alex became pastor and Raquel director for children at the church. What started with eight people gathered together in a living room, is now about 130 people strong and growing. And lives are being changed. Alex says, we always said the church was not about people coming to a service on Sunday morning, but about building relationships with those people. The whole point about what we believe is that the church is not about creating a big building where people come and sing a few songs and listen to a sermon. We believe church is a community of people who come together and are like-minded and want to do things together, eat together, visit each other's homes and have fun together. It's more about community than church services.

Alex tells the story of the early days of the church. There was a couple who did pretty well for themselves. In their mid-to-late 20's, they had kids, a single family home, but they were searching for things in life. They had issues with their family and their marriage. What we did was reach out to them. We held a root-beer kegger. We got a log cabin in the woods, invited a bunch of people and played root-beer pong, volleyball, other games, and just had a great time, trying to help them make a connection. It's not as if a keg party was going to solve all the issues, but it's a start. A way for this couple to have fun, to feel a connection with others like themselves, to feel a sense of community and find faith in life and provide a foundation for them to tackle their tougher issues. Connections like these are what the church tries to develop among all its members – fun and faith.

And it goes well beyond the church and its members. Alex says when the church started one of the things they wanted to do was to reach out and help people who aren't part of the church. Just a few years ago, Generation Church partnered with the Boys and Girls Club in Bel Air and provided winter coats and a movie for about 75 kids. When they first walked in the kids were hugging us and saying they had never been to the movies before, says Alex. I was amazed. These kids, 10, 11, 12 years of age who had never been to a movie theater. Some of them wore their coats during the entire movie. They were just so thrilled to have them and for the whole experience. That's why it's not just about Sunday morning and services, it's about helping these people and that if we weren't here, they wouldn't have these things, or this experience.

One of the complaints about churches in general, which Alex and the founding members heard time and time again – the church just wants my money. Two things the group decided to do to bring legitimacy to their efforts with Generation Church: number one—there is no donation plate passed during services. If members want to give, there is a basket in the back where they can donate. The second thing – there is no full-time staff, meaning no one earns a salary. This is a volunteer church. Alex earns his living helping others with insurance at WSMT in Bel Air, Maryland

and Raquel works as an Hispanic translator and secretary at Wolfe Street Academy in Baltimore.

The outreach of Generation Church even extends to the workplace. Just last week the church partnered with Raquel's school for a free sale. People from Generation Church donated items and families of the children who attended the school and others in the community could then come and take what they wanted. Members of Generation Church and the surrounding community donated three pick-up trucks full of stuff and twelve volunteers from the church donated their time to sort and distribute and then help pack everything up.

Alex says these are examples of things they do on a regular basis. Just this past summer, Generation Church sponsored a trip to Raquel's native land of Nicaragua and the church paid for children from a very poor town to attend camp. It was life affirming for so many.

On November 20th, Generation Church is sending 50 Thanksgiving Meals to two different elementary schools so the families can enjoy a holiday meal. And it is all made possible because of donations from church members.

Generation Church wants to reach people of all generations. Alex says, "we define generation as any person living at this time regardless of race, religion, or economic status. We want to help little kids, middle age, seniors, we think a healthy community is where all ages are involved, just like a family which is made up of multiple generations. And it's OK if this is not for everyone. We don't expect everyone to like our church," Alex says. "They can come to a service and decide it's not for them and that's OK with us. We are about helping people to find faith and hope in life and if we can be part of that journey, that is fantastic."

And Alex says there are two messages he wants to share: "The first is that for me as pastor, I believe that God has a plan for everyone's life and His plan is better than our plan. It's what I believe for my life. If not, I would just work and come home and not care. If people would just believe, they would be amazed." But he says there is a second, even more universal message for those who still might not agree with him and the message is this –"There is meaning and purpose to your life. There is hope for tomorrow and there is something you can follow and dream after, so don't give up."

Every generation blames the one before, and all of their frustrations come beating on your door.

–The Living Years, Mike & the Mechanics

Not at this door. The door is wide open for you. Generation Church wants to show you the way – sometimes all you need is a reason to believe.

Until next time, thanks for taking the time.

The Sunday Series: The Rain, The Pain...The Gain

You can do this, you have to do this. If you don't stand up today when are you going to stand? If the doctor says you can, then you must.

–Tim Kenney

They say in the world of real estate it's all about location, location, location. For realtor Tim Kenney, the place where his crash happened saved his life.

The Rain

It was raining so hard, just so hard on that Friday night, December 6th, 2013. When Tim completed his real estate settlement with his client at a Remax Real Estate office in Arbutus, Maryland, the two said a quick goodbye and then ran to their cars. The heavens had opened, the rain was coming down in buckets, and Tim's wipers were on high, as he struggled to see out of the windshield of his car. He pulled out of the parking lot and drove up a short hill, where he could see the blinking light. Tim had one desire on this Friday evening, he wanted to get home to his wife and two young children. But sometimes your greatest desire is thwarted by fate.

The flashing light at the top of the hill blinked red for Tim, and apparently yellow, as a caution light for cars coming from a different direction. That light is the last thing Tim Kenney remembers. The next details are those that have been told to him by family and the firefighters on the scene. No one still knows who was really at fault on that rain-drenched December night, but the reality of physics cannot be denied –a woman driving a Chevy Malibu, and traveling at a speed in excess of 50 mph plowed into Tim's BMW. In that single moment, his life changed forever.

The location of Tim's accident most assuredly saved his life. The crash happened within 400 feet of the Arbutus Volunteer Fire Department. Several firefighters heard the crash and ran to assist. The firefighters were at the scene within minutes of impact and within 15 minutes they used the jaws of life to extract Tim through the roof of his car. Within 45 minutes, he was at University of Maryland Shock Trauma.

From the picture above the next details I'm about to list for Tim's injuries almost make sense, the fact that he's even alive doesn't...it's nothing short of a miracle.

Tim's list of injuries: his left femur completely snapped in half, his pelvis broken on both sides, all of his ribs, crushed, the vertebrae in his back, broken, his left lung completely collapsed, his right lung at half its capacity, both kidneys failed, and the most serious injury – which a CAT scan confirmed at the hospital – the path to Tim's heart, his aorta, was torn and he was bleeding internally. From impact to Shock Trauma it had been a less than an hour, the next few hours would decide Tim's fate.

Tim's wife Paige was contacted by police, yet all they knew at the time was that her husband had a broken leg. But when she arrived the tests had been completed and the doctors shared the news. They told her Tim's condition was critical, they needed to arrange for emergency surgery to get a stint where the tear was in the aorta valve and stop the bleeding. Paige nearly passed out. The couple had two children at home, 3-year-old Taylor and 1-year-old Eloise. When news of the accident broke, Paige's mom rushed over to watch her grandchildren. Now Paige was at Shock Trauma and there lay her husband, basically on life support and the doctors telling her they "expected" he'd pull through. But they told Paige to go home to her young children, the team was being prepared and surgery wouldn't be until very early in the morning. When she arrived back home, it was her son Taylor, for some reason standing at the top of the stairs. In her mind, Paige was thinking the worst, there was a possibility Taylor and Eloise might grow up without their daddy, that's when she broke down.

Back at the hospital, it was now early morning and the surgeons were busy. Two operations at the same time – one to get the stint into Tim's aorta, the other to put his left leg back together. The heart surgery was a success, the bleeding stopped and at the same time the doctors inserted a 22-inch rod into Tim's left leg. His femur had broken perfectly into two pieces, so the rod would do the trick. Every other part of his body, the kidneys, the pelvis, the lungs, they would all have to heal on their own.

Tim's next memory is about a day later when he awoke in the hospital and saw Paige. He was still intubated, unable to talk or breathe on his own, but his arms and hands had been spared and with the dry erase board the nurses had given him he wrote down three letters and showed them to his wife: WTF.

Paige was just happy to see Tim's brain and hands working. In fact, all of his motor functions and brain functions were in good order, the doctors determined there was no paralysis. Later that same evening the tube was removed from Tim's throat and he was able to breathe on his own, an early celebration of what would be a long recovery. Tim was now stable, and although badly hurt, his mind was in good shape – he was aware. As he would soon learn it was a blessing...and a curse.

The Pain

Tim's body was simply crushed by the accident. "The first week in Shock Trauma it was all about the pain," says Tim. "I don't think anyone has experienced pain at this level. My whole body was broken, and when the nurses would come to move me, to clean me, or to change clothes, I had to stick a towel between my teeth, so I could scream at the top of my lungs every time they turned me. Even with the morphine and the Oxycontin they gave me 15-to-20 minutes before they came back to change the dressing, the pain was so extreme. The next five or six days, it was all about trying to get through the pain."

https://www.facebook.com/video.php?v=10151885745558800

There was a clock with a second-hand on the wall that Tim could see and it marked the excruciatingly slow passage of time. They say that time heals all wounds, but in this case, time was Tim's greatest enemy. Medication to fight the pain could only be given every three hours. The vicious cycle, repeated over and over, went something like this: the nurses would give Tim his pain meds and he would fall asleep, more like a drug-induced coma, for about an hour. He would awake in the second hour as the pain returned, in a pool of sweat and desperately wanting more meds. By the third hour, the pain became so intense Tim would just stare at the clock, the second-hand ticking every so slowly, until he could push the call button and at exactly the third hour, and not one minute later, to receive his medication.

Then the cycle would begin again.

After about a week in Shock Trauma, the physical therapist arrived. It was time to get out of bed. Just six months prior to this moment, Tim Kenney had finished a 600 mile trip on his road bike, The Ride the Rockies Bike Tour. Climbing the mountains on his road bike he thought there is no way a human can do this, ride uphill for three hours at a clip. For Tim that feeling was about to be surpassed by somehow getting his crushed body into an upright position and out of bed to walk, with the aid of a walker, over to a chair in the room. Tim says he first thought, "there is no way I can do this, it's going to hurt so bad." But he quickly used the mind over matter lessons he had learned in his ride through the Rockies –"you can do this, you have to do this. If you don't stand up today when are you going to stand? If the doctor says you can, then you must."

Tim did what he had to do. As a matter of fact, he kept working at it and within another week he was out of Shock Trauma and transferred to the Kernan Rehab Hospital. Tim says the pain was still a "10 out of 10," but he was so determined to get out and get back home to his family that in a three-day period of time – doing hours of rehab on his own, outside of what was required by the physical therapist –he accomplished the three goals which could secure his release: walk the 150 foot track at the rehab hospital three times, lift his damaged leg six inches off the ground and walk a set of stairs with his walker. Tim remembers calling Paige when the nurse signed off for him to go home. "I passed the test, I was crying, I called my wife and I could barely talk because I was so filled with emotion. It was December 18th, I thought I would be here for Christmas, but I was getting out!" With nearly a week to go before Christmas, Tim was back home.

"I don't know if I realized what was coming in terms of the real recovery," says Tim. "You go from trauma center, to surgery to post-surgery and a little bit of rehab progress to get home, then realize you still have a long way to go to be pain-free." While being home helped with the emotional pain of being away from his young family, the physical pain continued in its intensity. Tim could not sleep in his bed, the pain from his still-broken body was just too much. So for weeks, the only place he could bear to sit was on a love seat in his home, as the cycle of excruciating pain, pills, drug-filled sleep, (maybe 90 minutes at a clip), and more pain continued. Eventually, by mid-January, Tim says he started to feel better. The watershed moment came later that month when the doctor told Tim he could now use a cane and put 70% pressure on his left leg, and even drive.

...The Gain

Tim said he threw away the powerful pain pills, he didn't want to deal with them anymore. The day he got home from the doctor he told Paige he was heading out. She couldn't believe it. It had been snowing that day, so Tim switched from his cane to his snowshoes, even though it took him 40 minutes to get them on and even longer to stand up... and he headed out to go snowshoeing. "I was never so empowered," says Tim. "I felt like Superman. It was a turning point, the one where I knew I was in the process of healing and I can walk again. It made me feel like I was going to be OK."

Prior to that moment, Tim had proven himself to his family and friends by attending his kids' Christmas show at their school, albeit with his walker, and even attended the holiday work party for his real estate team. At every event those in attendance who had heard about the accident were astonished to see him out and about. But that's Tim Kenney – going above and beyond.

Tim says his goal for this summer is to heal to the point he can Ride the Rockies once again, 600 miles in seven days. Few doubt he won't make it there, certainly not his wife Paige. Tim says the support from his wife has been unbelievable. The couple has been married for eight years, but been together for nearly a decade-and-a-half. "She's my best friend," says Tim. "She is my everything. She is my partner, the mother of my children, she is incredible." He also says his parents, his family, aunts, uncles and the support of his closest friends has been amazing. Day after day during his 14-day stay at Shock Trauma, those who know him the best and love him the most would come by to see him. When a "bring a meal" opportunity was announced on social media, within the first hour the two-month calendar was completely filled.

Tim says he exercises and does rehab seven days a week now, trying to get all his body strength to return. He had lost 35 pounds after the accident, but he is doing a lot of strength training, cross training, hiking, cycling, snowshoeing and his goal is to be in the best shape of his life. Tim says he realized that exercise also helps his mind to heal. "I'm really focused on thinking," says Tim. "I think when I hike and I think about building up my business too. My real estate business actually grew while I was out of work. I have really good people working with me and we are preparing to have astronomical growth in 2015. Resiliency is one thing I really learned about myself. I don't know if I was ever really tested. I don't know in life if people really want to be tested."

Tim continues, "the one thing I learned is life throws you curves, you never know what is going to happen. You've got to pick yourself back up and get yourself back together, brush yourself off and do everything you can to get back to normal."

Words to live by, especially when you are simply grateful to live another day.

Until next time, thanks for taking the time.

About The Author

Mark Brodinsky is as a writer, blogger, author and inspirational speaker.

His first book *It Takes 2. Surviving Breast Cancer: A Spouse's Story*, chronicled the family's journey, as the mother of his children battled the beast back in 2012. The topic of breast cancer, shared from a spouse's perspective, helped make *It Takes 2*, a #1 Amazon Best-Seller in October, 2013.

From his Baltimore home, Mark writes a weekly blog: *It's Just About... Life & The Sunday Series*. During the week, the blog is a series of posts on personal development, inspiration and motivation. Each Sunday the blog focuses on the lives of other people, (maybe even yours), as Mark shares the stories of those he interviews, real people who demonstrate courage, give us hope and provide inspiration.

Mark's inspiration comes from watching his teenage daughters, Sophie and Emily, excel in the world – as well as from each and every person he speaks with – learning about their why and their way. He holds fast to his mission of positively impacting the lives of a billion people.

Mark also has a program of inspiration and motivation, *Lasting Change*, available to businesses looking to become more profitable, more productive and who want to increase employee or salesperson engagement and retention.

You can become one of the billion by reaching out to Mark at markbrodinsky@gmail.com, on social media (Facebook, Instagram, LinkedIn, Twitter) or clicking the Contact button on his website, www.markbrodinsky.com

www.ingramcontent.com/pod-product-compliance
Lightning Source LLC
Chambersburg PA
CBHW031502270326
41930CB00006B/215